Walking with God

Through
The Storm

A Daily Devotional
Study Journal

*Revealing the Light of Life
in times of darkness*

By Sarah Winbow

Walking with God through the Storm © 2020 Sarah Winbow. All rights reserved. No part of this publication may be reproduced, stored in a retrieval system or transmitted, in any form, or by any means, electronic, mechanical, photocopying, recording or otherwise, without the prior written permission of the author.

The emphasis given to Scriptures in bold type throughout this book is the author's. Scripture references are taken from the New International Version unless otherwise stated.

Scripture quotations taken from the HOLY BIBLE, NEW INTERNATIONAL VERSION. Copyright © 1973, 1978, 1984 by International Bible Society.

Used by permission of Hodder and Stoughton Publishers, A member of the Hodder Headline Group. All rights reserved. "NIV" is a registered trademark of International Bible Society. UK trademark number 1448790.

Music track *The Father Who Delights in You* © 2009 Living Seeds www.livingseeds.org Used by permission.

Cover: The Old Light, Lundy original water colour by Alan Mills.
Photo p.6 Shutterstock royalty-free stock photo ID: 1009139734.
Photo p.22 Shutterstock royalty-free stock photo ID: 1714769308.
Picture p.38 © Trinity House. Used by permission.
Photo p.52 Shutterstock royalty-free stock photo ID: 1086433550.
Photo p.66 Shutterstock royalty-free stock photo ID: 697841131.
Photo p.80 Shutterstock royalty-free stock photo ID: 562045069.
Photo p.94 Shutterstock royalty-free stock photo ID: 1226979577.
Photo p.104 Shutterstock royalty-free stock photo ID: 1360156673.
Poem p.108 Lundy's Ancient Light by Nicholas Szkiler. Used by permission.

ISBN 9781716906145

I would like to thank all those who piloted this material and also Alan & Chris Mills and Maggie Jones for all their help in the proof work and editing process.

To Alan and Chris Mills
You know that this would not have been written without you.
Thank you.

OTHER COURSES AND BOOKS BY SARAH WINBOW:

For those exploring Christianity, new believers or those who are stuck in their relationship with God:

> *Just the Beginning*
> *Simply Jesus*
> *Simply Jesus e-book*

> *Small Group Leader's Guides are available for both courses. Simply Jesus Leader's Guide is also available as an e-book.*

The Walking with God in Relationship Bible study series:

> *Prayer & God's Word*
> *Redeeming the Heart*
> *Soul & Strength*
> *Winning Your War*
> *The Baggage Checklist*

> *Small Group Leader's Guides are available for all courses.*

Other materials:

> *Set Free to Soar*
> *Restoring Eden*
> *Steps to Releasing your Community*
> *Biblical Feasts*

If you enjoy *Through the Storm* then please visit our website: www.newbeginningsdiscipleship.wordpress.com to read the testimonies. If the Lord gives you a testimony from working through this material then please get in touch through the website.

INTRODUCTION

We all face 'storms', they are inevitable to life. What matters is how we prepare ourselves beforehand in order to live through them and emerge on the other side.

The outbreak of Coronavirus across the world at the start of 2020 meant life as 'normal' for everyone changed. Our lives were turned upside down very suddenly as the people, jobs and routines that previously defined normality were removed. Whilst this virus will eventually disappear, other challenging situations will take its place. In each one the test for us is the same: how will we stand? Only a full assurance of who our God is and who He has called us to be through Jesus' blood will enable us to stand strong in Him as well as reach out an arm offering the certain hope of the gospel to others who are floundering.

These storms and challenges offer us real opportunities to shine the Light of Life we carry in our hearts but it will not shine if our foundation is unstable and we do not know the nature, promises, character and faithfulness of our covenant-keeping God. These things are the true hope of the gospel the people around us need too.

Some years ago, I found a photograph of a lighthouse standing strong in the midst of an angry swirling sea. The waves were so high they reached half-way up the side of the building. When I looked more closely, I could see the lighthouse keeper stood in the doorway with his arms folded and every appearance of calm and peace. This image really spoke to me and since then I have been taken on a journey with God which I now share with you in Through the Storm.

The devotional contains daily Bible readings, teaching and questions to prompt growth in your relationship with God. How you use it is up to you but you will need a Bible or Bible app, notebook and pen to write things down.

Sarah Winbow June 2020.

THE STORM
IT'S A STORMY WORLD...

DAY 1: THE LIGHTHOUSE

Read Exodus 33:12-23; Matthew 5:14-16.

I have a fascination with lighthouses! This probably stems from the fact that I was born and raised at the seaside. The literal meaning of the word 'lighthouse' is a fire tower and for centuries this is exactly what they were. Lighthouses tend to be constructed on solid rock and deliberately strong enough to withstand whatever severity of storm and sea-lashings the ocean throws up. Their light shines for the full 24 hours but it is only visible during the hours of darkness or the confusion of thick fog. The lighthouse's over-riding purpose at that time is to shine a light and sound a loud warning to prevent ships being wrecked and lives lost.

Whenever I mention the subject of lighthouses, people immediately jump to focus on the light but the truth is that without the careful construction of the tower itself - its foundation on the rock, the internal steps and different levels built gradually from ground-level upwards - the lighthouse would not be able to do its essential work.

In 2012 a small group of us spent part of a week on retreat on Lundy Island. On the evening before we were taken off-island I climbed to the top of the old abandoned lighthouse and stood on the former lamp platform. I was alone and simply began to worship God. As I did so I became aware of something like smoke hovering around and above my head. It being February and cold, I tested whether this was just my breath but it persisted even when I stopped singing. A friend walked up to join me from the harbour and as he arrived, he told me to quickly put the light out because it could be a distraction to shipping. There had been no light other than me!! It seems that as I gave myself unreservedly in worship to God and rededicated myself to be a beacon and fire-igniter for His Kingdom, He had supernaturally lit me up as a fire tower!! My friend just happened to have two candles and matches in his breast pocket (as you do!!) so we placed the candles on the lamp platform and lit them. We felt they represented the whole house of Israel: Jews and the Gentile church. What happened next took us both by surprise: through the magnification of the glass in the windows of the lamp room we saw these two tiny lights spread outwards not only across the whole island but further across the Bristol Channel into the South West, Wales and beyond towards the Irish Sea. There were literally hundreds upon hundreds of lights, so many it was impossible to count them.

On that extraordinary evening the Lord used these supernatural events to begin teaching me the profound prophetic symbolism of the lighthouse. Over the next few weeks, we will unpack this teaching together. We will begin by ensuring we have a strong foundation built solidly on Jesus the Rock. Then we will move gradually through the construction of the lighthouse until eventually we reach the lamp room and the light itself. This is necessarily a step-by-step process but if we want His burning light to shine brightly through us as we face one of the most uncertain and stormy seasons the world and the church have ever experienced, we need to pay careful attention to how we build. If we miss even one step then what is built will be faulty and therefore liable to subsidence or collapse. We need to nurture patience and allow Him to so build Himself in us and us in Him that He not only becomes our firm foundation but also our strong tower; a living breathing reality literally burning in our heart. Only then will we be able to remain strong, stable and secure through the fierceness of the storm. The end-result will be that the world around us will not only see the strength of His burning glory shining in us but also come to understand that Jesus is their light and hope too.

Additional reading: John 11:9; Acts 26:17-18; 2 Corinthians 3:7-18.

His will is for us to shine with His light and burn with His glory through the storms we face. Express your willingness to allow God to do whatever He needs to do in you to make you the person you need to be.

DAY 2: STORMS ARE INEVITABLE

Read John 16:33; Luke 8:22-25.

60's singer Lynn Anderson once sang *"I beg your pardon I never promised you a rose garden, along with the sunshine there's gotta be a little rain sometime."* Jesus warns us that whilst we live in this world, we must expect difficult stormy times. I wish it were not true but it is.

In the natural world there are many different grades of storm and this is also true for us in life. One person deals with the daily trials of caring for a loved one who, owing to dementia, is wandering the streets at night and constantly phoning the police whilst their neighbour's daughter arrives home to stay with nothing but a bag and her baby; another person struggles to deal with crippling anxieties, suicidal thoughts and a minimal level of self-confidence whilst their friend's over-confidence means they thoughtlessly blunder into situations stirring up unnecessary trouble and causing offence. The peace of our life can be suddenly overturned as we have to make sense of and live with the result of sudden job loss, relationship breakdown, accidents, traumas or other people's choices that impact our lives. Everyday matters like health, food, money, jobs, housing and family relationships mean we all have to live with storms.

Of course, I do not know what particular storm you are facing or living through right now but God does. It is not a surprise to Him and even though it may not feel like it, Jesus is with you; right in the centre of it with you. It is not the storm that is the issue but your reaction to it that matters: in everything we have a choice - either to let it overwhelm us and be damaged or broken by it or to place our trust in God. The name Jesus or *Yeshua* in Hebrew means 'salvation' or 'deliverer' so when we call on His name, even though the situation may remain the same and we still have to deal with it, deep inside He will bring calm to our anxious thoughts, maybe give us fresh guidance or reveal a solution. Over and above these things, He will bring our spirits to the place of peace in Him.

Additional reading: 2 Corinthians 4:8-18; Isaiah 43:1-2.

PRAYER TIME:

Reflect on your life today and make a list of any situations or circumstances you consider to be your current storms.

- *Which is the most pressing matter?*
- *What is Jesus saying to you?*

Pour your heart out to God over the most pressing storm you are facing. Thank Him that He understands. Thank Him that even though you still have to face the storm, He has promised to be with you in it. Ask Him to fill you with His peace and to teach you how to live as an overcomer.

DAY 3: THE END-TIME 'STORM'

Read Matthew 24.

Whilst it is very true that we are all tested and challenged by our own storms, we do not live our lives in isolation. There is always a context for our daily lives. As believers in Jesus that context should be defined by the constant expectation of His return. Jesus outlined a relatively short but fiercely intense time of sifting in the nations that must precede His coming. The apostles expected His imminent return and this expectation has been repeated throughout history: during the Crusades and Reformation, during the reign of Catholic Queen 'Bloody' Mary and during Cromwell's Commonwealth. Persecution of God-fearing believers has always been a sign for those living in this expectation.

When I first became a Christian in the early 1970s it was a time of great expectation. As a teenager Hal Lindsay's apocalyptic book, *The Late Great Planet Earth* terrified me that the end of the world was imminent. The upside was it was absolutely normal for Christians to go round telling people *"Jesus is coming back!"* We wore the T-shirts and had the psychedelic stickers on our Bibles declaring the same message! During the 80s and 90s things changed: if we preached about the Second Coming, we were almost an embarrassment. Perhaps we had become too sophisticated to believe in such things any more…

Whilst on retreat on Lundy in February 2005 I clearly heard the Lord say *"There's a storm coming."* I immediately knew God was not referring to an actual storm hitting land but He was speaking to me of the 'great storm' prophesied in scripture (i.e., the Day of the Lord) that is coming on the whole world – not just the British Isles. On that retreat I came to understand this would not be just one event but an intensifying storm which will see us live through a whole series of seemingly natural, ecological, economic, social and political circumstances, events and outcomes that will eventually have considerable consequences on how we are allowed to live our daily lives and especially as Christians how we are able to practise and live out our faith. Every aspect of modern society will be severely tested and shaken. Persecution is not something that happens to people elsewhere; it is already here. Our civil liberties to speak and live out our faith are already undermined in our laws.

Additional reading: Daniel 12:1-4; 1 Thessalonians 5:1-11.

PRAYER TIME:

Reflect on all you have read today.

- *How do you feel about this time?*
- *Are you afraid?*
- *Do you want to hide or run away?*
- *Do you hope to be able to stand through it?*

Write down any thoughts or questions you have.

Talk to Father God about your feelings. Ask Him to fill you with His peace and to teach you how to grow strong in Him.

DAY 4: REACTIONS

Read the story of Noah in Genesis 6-8; Luke 17:26-33.

As I write the *whole world* is in complete lockdown by Coronavirus. Anything like normal life has been suspended for an unknown period of time. This pandemic alone means the whole world lives with an uncertain economy, food shortages, job losses, enforced social changes and upheavals; hundreds of thousands of people being forced by circumstances to face many different types of storms.

Unfortunately, being a believer is no immunization from life's experiences. People repeatedly ask me *"Why is this happening to me?"* The hard-hearted truth is that unless we have faced our own storm head-on, been tested and stood strong in God through it, then how can we possibly hope to be a help to others through the greater storm that is increasingly being seen in the whole world. Be certain, everything society holds dear - our homes, families, churches, finances, pension funds, health care, education, police and justice systems - EVERYTHING that comprises society as we know it will be shaken by this end-time storm.

Not only are all these storms practical and personal but we also need to recognise we are facing a spiritual storm which requires a spiritual response. It would be perfectly understandable if we were to feel we do not have any spare capacity for this but that is exactly how the people living around Noah reacted. They were so focused on their own affairs they ignored the warnings.

Additional reading: 1 Peter 4:12; Romans 8:13-39.

PRAYER TIME:

Reflect on today's reading.

- *What aspects of modern society can you identify that were also prevalent in the days of Noah and Lot?*
- *What was the outcome for Noah's neighbours?*
- *Why would a loving heavenly Father allow such a severe judgement?*
- *Do we have a responsibility to warn people about the end-time storm?*

Noah's family was not saved from the storm - they still had to live through it - but through Noah's obedience they were protected from it. By God's mercy and grace, they were given victory over it. Talk to God about the things on your heart where you long to see the victory.

DAY 5: RESHAPING IS NECESSARY

Read Matthew 25; Luke 5:36-39.

On a return visit to Lundy with a small team of people in February 2012 the Lord repeatedly emphasised to us that the institutional church in our nation was on the rocks; at some point it would collapse and break up and this would be God's doing. In an extraordinary joint waking vision two of our number saw an earthquake split the floor of the parish church and EVERYTHING in the structure of the institution that had become the church - the pulpit, choir stalls, altar, reredos, font etc. - fell into the chasm. It crumbled at its foundations. The Lord said there would be no mending of the situation; the old outdated structure would be brought to complete wreckage in order for a new shape to emerge.

We understood God was showing us that at some point the church itself would experience such a pruning and re-shaping that it would no longer look, think or act the same as before. It would no longer be an organisation but a living breathing organism characterised by unconditional love and compassion rather than ritual or liturgy; believers would become Kingdom-minded rather than church-building focused and be found more on the streets and gathered in small groups in homes instead of traditional buildings. No-one could have foreseen the suddenness with which the beginning of this re-shaping has come about through the Coronavirus lockdown.

This vision of the reshaped church was given at the *exact same time* as I was being lit up like a beacon in the Old Light (see Day 1). As we came together afterwards and shared our remarkable stories, we came to understand the message: those who had learned the importance of obedience to Father's moment-by-moment leading would become like beacons of hope and light in the midst of the increasing darkness and so directing those they met into the safety, security and refuge of the

Lighthouse i.e., a relationship with God through Jesus. However, this Holy Spirit led, counter-culture activity, would lead to increasing levels of opposition both from the established institutional church trying desperately to save itself from collapse as well as from wider secular society.

Additional reading: Acts 2:38-47.

PRAYER TIME:

Reflect on **Matthew 25:1-13.**

- *What is this referring to? Who is the Bridegroom?*
- *Who are the virgins?*
- *Is this speaking of a wholly practical preparation like Noah's or might the oil be representative of something else; if so then what?*
- *Could this be related to why the church must be re-shaped?*

Talk to God about the challenges He has shown you.

DAY 6: THE LIFEBOAT

Read Hebrews 12:26-29.

It is sobering to consider that our loving Father God can also be a destructive all-consuming fire whose holiness, righteousness and justice are not to be taken lightly and whose Word is not to be messed with or disregarded. Why would He allow such a severe judgement? The answer is simple: in order to humble the hearts of a rebellious and disobedient people in the hope they will turn back to Him. He wants heart-relationship not just religious activity.

The Bible is full of stories illustrating how His children experienced difficult trials in order that they should turn back to Him. You will already know the truth of this from your own life-journey. What is different now is the context: this level of shaking has never before happened on the world-wide scale that we see today. Only once since the creation of the earth has the whole world been locked down, unable to carry on normal life; this was the flood in the time of Noah.

In order not only to survive but also to reach out offering the certainty of hope in God to the hundreds of thousands of people who will cry to Him in their humbled circumstances we need a different type of boat altogether: something that has a very different shape. This spiritual lifeboat will be prepared and equipped to respond when the call comes to be part of God's rescue plan. In order for us to be the people He needs us to be, to do the work He means us to do, we need to prepare ourselves. This involves learning how to know Him more, to live strong in Him and to live as overcomers through our own personal storms because only then will we be able to hold out an arm offering the living hope of a relationship with God through Jesus to others.

Additional reading: Isaiah 42:5-9; 1 Peter 3:15.

PRAYER TIME:

Reflect on today's reading.

- *Have you ever imagined you could possibly be the generation that witnessed Jesus' return?*

Write down your thoughts and fears.

- *How do you respond to God's invitation to get involved?*
- *What might a modern-day spiritual lifeboat look like?*

Write down what you think this might mean for you.

Talk to Father God about your feelings. Ask Him to fill you with His peace and to prepare you in every way for your role.

DAY 7: ARISE AND SHINE

Read Isaiah 32:1-8; 60:1-3; Matthew 5:14-16.

God never meant His church to be an organisation that would restrict the ability of His Body to truly function in the fullness and flexibility of its giftings and ministries. During the Coronavirus lockdown the church has suddenly been catapulted out of its buildings and back into homes. Fellowship, community and our personal relationship with God have become more important than ritual and religious exercises. What the Lord is doing in this reshaping is removing our dependency on our buildings and even the good things we do for Him; He is refocusing our priority simply onto Him. He wants us - wholeheartedly, completely and unreservedly. When this is true of us then we will also understand what it means to have Him in all His fullness. When we have learned to find our rest in Him and draw our strength from His presence then we will be able to overcome in our spirits ANY storm that is thrown at us - those from our past, from our inward fears and insecurities, in our homes, families, businesses or from the state. Daniel writes concerning these times:

"...the people who know their God shall be strong, and carry out great exploits."[1]

Essentially the whole of this week's readings and teaching has been setting the scene, for it is entirely possible we are experiencing the birth-pains the Bible says will immediately precede Jesus' return. Jesus declared Himself to be the Light of the World[2] but today's reading shows how He passed that responsibility onto us. So, our end goal is to live secure in Him as fearless overcomers and to so burn with the Spirit of God that the Light

---

[1] Daniel 11:32b N.K.J.V.
[2] John 8:12; 9:4-5.

He has placed within us becomes obvious to those around us. When they look at us, they no longer see anything of our humanity but Him instead. When we say *"Jesus Christ is our living hope"* they can see it to be true from our face and demeanour. That type of light is a very powerful witness and is attractive to draw others to the Light without even trying. It emits the warning of authenticity that terrifies the enemy who operates in the darkness. It illuminates Jesus and clearly points those who are seeking to find the living Way, Truth and Life for themselves.

Additional reading: 1 Peter 1: 3-25.

PRAYER TIME:

This is the life I know I need to live in this season.

- *How about you?*
- *Are you ready to follow the steps to allow God to build His Lighthouse in you?*

Write down your feelings and turn them into your prayer of dedication.

BEDROCK
RECOGNISING WHO IS ON OUR SIDE

The light that shines from the lamp room of a lighthouse is not the beginning but the end result of a building process. The lighthouse has to be constructed from the ground upwards with its foundations set firmly on solid rock...

DAY 8: THE LORD IS MY ROCK

Read Psalm 18 especially verse 2; Proverbs 18:10.

Princess Diana famously dubbed her servant Paul Burrell her 'rock'. Since her death history has proven that despite his loyalty to her whilst she lived, even he was flawed. In fact, no human being can ever be our 'rock'; we are all imperfect with unsound motives and inconsistent character traits. Sooner or later, we are bound to do something to disappoint, hurt or offend. When we lose our 'rock' what do we do then?

I was brought up in the West Country and thought I had seen some pretty big rocks in glorious Cheddar Gorge along with the great boulders of Stonehenge and Avebury Ring but in 2015 I was introduced to a rock of a completely different proportion: The Rock of Gibraltar. The Rock dominates the tiny isthmus that links the city to mainland Spain. Its huge strategic significance at the gateway to the Mediterranean has meant it has been fought over and disputed for centuries. It became a British Overseas Territory in 1713. From that time on the British military began to tunnel inside the Rock and during WWII this tunnel network was expanded to such a degree that there are now approximately **33 miles** of tunnel **inside** the Rock of Gibraltar!

My host knew the person who controls all that happens within the Rock and he agreed to take us inside and show us things that are definitely not on the regular tourist route e.g., there are two hospitals, military kitchens and emergency accommodation for up to 22000 people and we were also told of vehicles, planes, missiles, bank vaults and gold bars all hidden away from plain sight inside the Rock.

The visit had a profound effect on me as I began to compare the significance of what I had seen with what the Bible teaches about the Lord: one of His names is Rock. Prior to my Gibraltar visit I had only seen the Rock as something I might stand **on** i.e., on the outside. My visit inside the

Rock of Gibraltar showed me a completely different perspective: hidden inside was everything needed for refuge and security in a time of war or upheaval. If we, during this season where we all face our personal storms, will take the time and make the effort to spiritually tunnel deeper into our relationship with God - to do in the spiritual what the military did in the natural, we will have a deeper understanding of who He really is. As the strength of the storms we face increase, we will find we can be truly confident and secure in Him. **Everything** we need has already been provided in Him, our Rock. To gain access to Him is not a hard or dangerous climb to the top because, like the tunnels in Gibraltar, all the access is on ground level; all we need to do is walk on in!

Additional reading: Deuteronomy 33:12; Psalms 31:1-3; 61:1-4; 91.

PRAYER TIME:

Look back at the different types of things that are stored inside the Rock of Gibraltar.

- *Do any of these speak to you of other names of God?*
- *Can you find any scriptures where He gives Himself that name?*
- *How have these insights affected your perspective on God's loving kindness, faithfulness and care of you?*
- *What does this say to you about any other 'rock' you may have been trusting in?*
- *Does He seem bigger?*

Spend some time talking to Him about all He has shown you today.

DAY 9: I AM WHO I AM

Read Exodus 3 especially verse 14.

Moses had been raised in Pharaoh's palace and yet he was working as a humble shepherd in the desert when God seriously intervened in his life. For 430 years the Hebrews had been enslaved in Egypt[3] and no doubt Moses, like the rest of his people, had been crying out to God for deliverance. What He would not have anticipated is that God meant to use *him* to make it happen. In fact, his whole life had been ordered by God to prepare him to have the favour to access Pharaoh's presence. Yet He doubted the call and his abilities to fulfil the task.

Just as in the days of Noah and Moses, God has a plan to use us, His children, to bring refuge, deliverance and salvation to the communities where we live. Moses was so locked-in to the daily task of caring for the sheep that he could not see who he was in God's eyes or the enormity of who the God who simply described Himself as *"I AM WHO I AM"*[4] was either. He needed a shift in perspective because without it, he would not be able to arise and shine in the way God intended him to do. This is equally true for us today. As precious children of God we have choices: we can choose to be confined or consumed by our daily situations and personal storms or we can choose instead to allow the Holy Spirit to lift us up to gain Father's wider (and often longer-term) perspective. This is not some form of Christian escapism; actually, it is the complete opposite. Father God knows the hairs on our head, the people we have to deal with, the problems we face and our very serious worries and He longs to be

---

[3] Exodus 12:40.
[4] Exodus 12:11.

included in it all so that we might experience the strength, warmth and comfort of the reality of His embrace.

Many years ago, when I first began to learn Hebrew, I well remember the modest thrill I got in translating a sentence into English and realising that when God applied the words 'I AM' to Himself, He really was using the verb 'to be'! His name, that is written in Mazoretic text as יהוה *[Y/H/W/H]* and was pronounced in the time of Moses as something like *Yahweh*, means *'I am'* or *'I will be'*! In calling Himself *'I AM'* God is actually saying:

'I am or will be here for you – always. Wherever you go, through whatever you face, I will always be with you. In times of blessing or in times of difficulty you will never be alone – I am now and will always be your constant I AM.'

Additional reading: Psalm 7; Isaiah 55:9.

PRAYER TIME:

- *How did David's perspective of God change in Psalm 7?*
- *What is God teaching you about Himself?*
- *What is He showing you about yourself?*

Spend a longer time with God today. Identify one particular need or situation and consciously bring it before Him. As you worship allow Him to lift you up over it.

DAY 10: ENDURING LOVE 1

Read Genesis 12: 1-5; 1 John 3:1.

Have you ever sat on a sunny seat or wall, pointed your head skyward and just basked in the balmy warmth of the sun on your face? The naked strength of this heat is a metaphor that allows us to glimpse just a fraction of the fierce intensity of God's love towards us. Whatever benefit and blessing we feel from the sun's warmth, it is just a minute fraction of the lavish loving-kindness constantly flowing earthwards from the sun's Creator God. He loves and cares deeply for us. That is the truth. It is a truly awesome thing that we as individuals can know Father God's heart of love for us intimately and personally. But the story of the Bible, from the Garden of Eden right through to the end of Revelation, reveals that Father's heart of love is not only towards individuals, but also to nations.

In Genesis 12 God called one nomadic man, Abram, to follow Him, which he did obediently and faithfully. God valued Abram's humble heart to such an extent that He entered into a covenant relationship with him whereby He promised childless and rootless Abram multitudes of descendants with a homeland of their own. Genesis 16 relates the story of how by using Hagar, Abram tried to make it happen himself. The result of her pregnancy was Ishmael, the father of the Arabic peoples. After his birth God changed Abram's name to Abraham meaning 'father of many'. In the face of Abraham's apparent moral failure, we might have been tempted to walk away from the relationship but Genesis 17 describes how God did not do that, instead He affirmed the covenant He had made.

In Genesis 18:10 an angelic visitor prophesied to Abraham that within a year his wife Sarah, who was way past child-bearing age, would give birth to her own son. She laughed at the prospect but true enough within the year Isaac (ironically meaning laughter) was born. Through Isaac's descendants the blood-line of the Hebraic people is traced. The remainder of the book of Genesis tells the story of how Abraham's family grew from one family into a whole nation and how they came to be living in slavery to Pharaoh in Egypt.

Additional reading: Psalm 100:5; 106:1; 107:1; 118:1.

PRAYER TIME:

- *Who initiated the covenant with Abram?*
- *What do you think the significance of this might be?*

In the Hebrew texts of the additional reading there is actually no word in any of the passages that is translated into English as 'endures'. It simply says 'God loves forever'. The word 'endure' has been inserted by translators.

- *Can you think why they have done this?*

Spend time meditating on God's enduring Father-heart of love. Pour out your heart of thanksgiving to Him.

DAY 11: ENDURING LOVE 2

Read Exodus chapters 19, 20 & 32.

On Day 9 we considered how God used Moses to deliver His people from slavery in Egypt. He brought them out in order for them to be set apart exclusively to Him. Exodus 19:1-8 outlines how at Mount Sinai God and the Israelites were effectively betrothed to one another. In the remainder of chapter 19 God told His bride to prepare herself to come and meet Him up close, in the intimacy of the mountain (the trumpets are a traditional part of a Jewish wedding that announce the imminent arrival of the bridegroom). The people were terrified by the noise, smoke and fire and begged Moses to go up and meet God as their representative, which he did. Whilst he was there God gave Moses the terms of the marriage contract – the 10 Commandments (moral and civil guidelines so that Israel could live as the kind of bride He intended her to be) – and the instructions for the tabernacle which represents the marital home where bride and groom would regularly meet together.

Whilst Moses was with God the faithless people were already committing adultery! At first, God was grieved and angry but Moses pleaded for forgiveness and v.14 of chapter 32 says *"The Lord relented"*. In chapter 34:5-8 we read how God came down powerfully and met intimately with Moses, again re-affirming over and over His faithful and enduring love for His chosen people. Truly Father God loves forever.

After a period of 40 years wandering in the desert i.e., until the original rebellious group brought out of Egypt had died off, God eventually took His people into the long-Promised Land. Joshua led the people in successive victories but after his death Israel struggled to keep the land they had gained. The book of Judges depicts years of cyclical behaviour: the people sinned, God raised up a leader (judge), they repented and turned back to Him for a while; the people sinned, et.al. Eventually we read in Judges 17:6: *"In those days Israel had no king; everyone did as he saw fit."* It seems that without a human intermediary the people were incapable of faithfully following God for themselves.

Additional reading: Judges 17:6 & 21:25.

PRAYER TIME:

Reflect on all you have learned today.

- *In what ways has your perception of Father God's heart of covenant love grown?*

Spend some time thanking and worshipping God that forever He loves and that He has, forever, loved you.

DAY 12: ENDURING LOVE 3

Read 1 Samuel 8:6-20; Psalm 137.

After the period of the judges God raised up prophets to speak to the people on His behalf, but, again, this did not satisfy them. We cannot say they were not warned of the consequences (they were!) BUT because of His great love for them, God agreed to give them a human king to be their leader just like the other nations.

Saul was a natural leader but failed because he was more of a people-pleaser than a God-pleaser. He did not follow God whole-heartedly. David was both a natural and a gifted leader; he was also totally determined, with a passionate heart of love, to be obedient to God. Whilst David reigned under God, Israel became so wealthy and mighty that when his son Solomon inherited on David's death, he became king over the richest, most successful, powerful and blessed nation ever to have existed. But Solomon fell away; he married foreign wives with occult backgrounds and practices which seriously displeased God's heart. From then onwards Israel began to lose its wealth; David's sons fell out with each other with the result that the kingdom was divided. Eventually they were overrun by the Babylonians who firstly besieged Jerusalem, then ransacked it, completely destroying Solomon's magnificent temple. The inhabitants of the city were then carried off into captivity in Babylon where, with hindsight, they mourned for what they had lost.

Despite the whole sad and sorry history, Father God still loves His people forever. His covenant love has certainly endured through much pain and rejection and deep in His heart God continued to search for a people who would love Him, and be obedient to Him. Much of what is written in the prophetic books of the Old Testament points to the next stage of God's awesome love and grace-fuelled plan and at exactly the right time for the Jewish people, politically, socially, economically and spiritually, God sent

His precious only Son, Jesus, into the world to *"save His people from their sins"*[5]. Jesus' name in Hebrew is Yeshua. It derives from the verb 'to save' and means 'one who saves', 'saviour' or 'deliverer'. Jesus was the long-promised Messiah, Anointed One, who would be the physical agent and expression of God's covenant love on earth.

Additional reading: Galatians 4:4-7; 3:6-9; Romans 5:1-11; Ephesians 2:11-3:6.

PRAYER TIME:

Write down some of the many ways you know Jesus demonstrated, illustrated and manifested Father's heart of covenant love towards His people.

- *What was the eventual outcome for us?*
- *How does this relate to God's covenant love relationship?*

Reflect on all you have read and thought about today. Give thanks to God for including you in His covenant love relationship through Jesus. Pray for those you love who still need to know Jesus for themselves.

---

[5] Matthew 1:21.

DAY 13: OUR COVENANT PARTNER

Read Genesis 15.

In order to gain a greater understanding of the depth of God's enduring love for us and what it really means when His Name *'I AM'* indicates He will always be there for us, we need to look deeper into what is indicated by the term 'covenant relationship'.

In simple terms 'covenant' means two parties enter into a binding agreement, contract, pledge, treaty, or bond.[6] In biblical times covenant relationships were something practised by many people groups and would certainly have involved the shedding of blood in some form. Therefore, it was a profoundly solemn and sacred ritualistic way of expressing deep levels of care, trust and friendship as well as forming alliances to keep the peace between tribes and nations. Culture has changed so much over time that the only form of true covenant that Western nations understand today is that of marriage and even that has been diluted to such an extent we can now be granted a quickie divorce within 6 months. Modern society no longer understands the rich symbolism of the covenant ceremony either, which means we can easily overlook what the Bible has to teach us about the sheer depth of Father's love for us. Richard Booker in *The Miracle of the Scarlet Thread*[7] outlines nine steps to making covenant, each carried out by both parties:

RITUAL:	SYMBOLISM:
1. Remove coat & hand over.	Everything I am, I give to you.
2. Remove belt used to keep armour in place & hand over.	My battles are yours: I will defend, protect and fight for you.

---

[6] Windows Office 2010 Thesaurus
[7] Pp.27-31 Booker, 1981, Sounds of the Trumpet Inc. ISBN 0-914903-26-8.

3.	Cut the animal into two halves down the middle; lay flat on the ground. Walk in figure of 8 (symbolic of making a new beginning) and come back to face each other.	I am dying to myself; giving up all rights to my own life and making a new beginning with you my covenant partner.
4.	Raise right arm & mix blood.	The intermingling of blood states our lives have become one life.
5.	Exchange names.	We take each other's last names as our own names.
6.	Make a scar.	The scar left where our blood was mixed is the seal or guarantee of the covenant. Those seeing the scar instantly know we are in a covenant relationship.
7.	Give covenant terms.	We publicly state that whatever is mine is yours and vice versa, both assets and liabilities.
8.	Eat a memorial meal.	We eat bread and wine representing our own flesh and life-blood. We are stating 'My blood is your blood; my flesh is your flesh'. We are in life together.
9.	Plant a lasting memorial.	Commonly this was a tree sprinkled with the blood of the animal. From now on we would be known as friends.

Additional reading: Isaiah 61:10; 2 Chronicles 20:15-17; Galatians 2:20; 2 Corinthians 1:21-22; John 6:54-56; Luke 9:23; John 15:14-15.

- *How has what you have learned reshaped your perspective of God's ability to stand with you through any storms you might face?*

DAY 14: COVENANT BLOOD

Read Isaiah 53; Jeremiah 31:31-33; Hebrews 12:18-29.

Even a quick scan over the 9 steps (Day 13) shows how important sacrifice - the shedding of actual blood - was to covenant-making. From our much sanitized 21st Century perspective this can seem a bit gruesome and archaic but in order to understand this we need to ask two questions: *'Why is blood so important'* and *'What does blood do?'*

Blood is essential to life. Blood circulation is controlled by the beating of our heart, which is why when our heart stops the blood stops pumping and we die. As blood circulates it delivers essential substances to our cells e.g., oxygen, hormones and various proteins and nutrients[8]. At the same time, it cleanses those same cells from all waste products like carbon dioxide, urea and lactic acid. It fights disease, signals tissue damage, regulates our body's temperature and coagulates to prevent us bleeding to death every time we have a scratch.

Blood is an amazingly complex, wonderful creation of a loving Father God who takes life and death very seriously. So, when animals were sacrificed and their blood poured out to mark the sealing of a covenant or onto an altar as an act of worship, applied to doorposts as a prophetic sign that this house is under God's protection or sprinkled on the priests and people as a sign their sins are forgiven and they are cleansed, then its meaning in the heart of God goes far deeper and is more profound than we can possibly imagine or understand.

The spread of the Bible from beginning to end shows how every part of the covenant ritual symbolism is fulfilled in Jesus. The magnitude of God's faithful, enduring unconditional love for us meant that ultimately, He would plant a covenant memorial 'tree' at the Cross in His own flesh as the

---

[8] Glucose, amino acids and fatty acids et. al.

final blood sacrifice. Jesus' body and blood is the fulfilment of *every* sin offering throughout the Old Testament. Jesus' sacrificial death is the 'blood of the New Covenant' mentioned in Jeremiah 31:31-33 which is for everyone not just the Israelites.

The blood of Jesus does exactly the same for us spiritually as our own blood does for us naturally: His blood cleanses us of all impurities which today's reading in Isaiah reminds us includes the limitations of sicknesses and diseases. The covenant exchange means His life-giving blood, full of spiritual oxygen and every single spiritual protein and nutrient brings us the potential for complete wholeness and health. This exchange should affect and influence who we are and how we live because EVERYTHING we might ever need for life is found in His blood. Every promise, every aspect of His character, the fulfilment and truth of every single Name God has ever revealed Himself to be is found in the blood of Jesus. We no longer have to bring blood offerings and smear blood on our faces or houses because our relationship with God is now based on applying the fullness of all He is to the spiritual doorposts of our hearts and lives by faith through prayer.

He is who He says He is. He is the bedrock. He is *'I AM.'*

Additional reading: Exodus 24:1-10; Zechariah 9:9-17; 1Corinthians 11:23-26; Hebrews 13:20-21.

PRAYER TIME:

Everything you need to help you is found in Him. It is underserved - a complete gift of grace. The wonderful truth is it is yours to appropriate in your own life by faith in the covenant blood of Jesus.

- *Can you make the choice to trust Him to be with you through it?*

Talk to Him about it all.

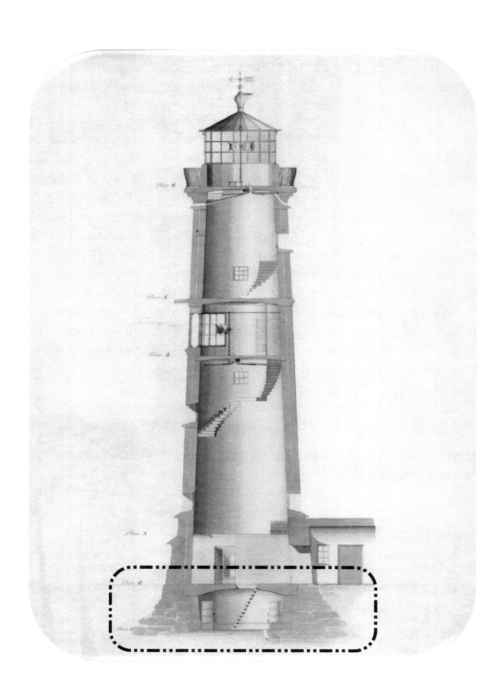

FOUNDATIONS
PREPARING TO KNOW HIM BETTER

The very real temptation is to get straight on with construction of the building but in order to go higher we must first go lower...

DAY 15: DOWN TO THE BARE ROCK

Read Luke 6:46-49.

A lighthouse has to be built on solid rock. Speaking spiritually this bedrock is our covenant relationship with God.

Sometimes it literally took three or four years of battling against the continual power and fierceness of stormy seas and ferocious winds before bedrock foundations were sufficiently strong and stable enough for upward building to begin. Once these foundations were in place, building the tower was the easy part; this would often be completed in one short building season. The temptation for us all is to want to press on with the building. Nobody really likes the hard work of digging foundations but just as the lighthouse pioneers had to persist and endure through the storms they faced, we also need to learn how to dig down deep into our relationship with Him in order to endure through the storms that hit us.

It does not matter if we are rich or poor, black or white, Jew or Gentile – the ups and downs of life's storms happen to us all. Some are the kind we can pray into and know we have received the breakthrough because the storm disappears but the truth is that many of us live with storms that just do not go away. How we react, cope with and face these storms boils down to the type of spiritual foundations we have in place. We need to have proved His constant love and faithfulness through our personal storms now, so that when bigger storms hit, we should be able not only to stand strong ourselves but also reach out, offering the gospel of true hope to others. Not one of us can say with any certainty that we *WILL* stand under such immense testing; we hope that we will but we may not. Faced with the seriousness of this we must be willing to take whatever steps we can to mature in the things of God. Theory, theology and head knowledge are all well and good but we need more than this. A day is coming when it will no longer be sufficient just to say or sing the right things or raise our hands at the right moment; we will need to truly *KNOW HIM* and have proved Him faithful through our experience of Him at work in our everyday lives.

I thought I had a pretty solid relationship with God until I received the diagnosis that I had a serious incurable auto-immune disease that could, in time, affect and kill-off the ability of my blood vessels, muscles, and internal organs to function normally. To say I was stunned is an understatement but I was glad to receive an explanation for the symptoms that had been developing in my body over the previous four years. Despite my efforts to stand strong in the Lord my mind began to be bombarded with all sorts of fearful, negative and harmful thoughts. As I gave into these, there was an increase in the manifestation of the different symptoms. Months went by when I struggled to get through the day because I felt so ill. I knew I was not right. I also knew that if I continued getting worse then I did not stand even half a chance of fulfilling all I believe God has planned for me in the season of the greater storm up ahead. So, I went to my Father God and told Him all of this...

Additional reading: 1 Corinthians 2:13; Psalm 127:1.

PRAYER TIME:

- *What does the bare rock signify in terms of your relationship with God?*
- *Is it possible to lay down such an inward foundation in Jesus that it remains secure and firm through the severest of testing storm? How can you begin to dig-down deeper?*
- *What is the Lord teaching you about Himself?*
- *What is He showing you about yourself?*

Talk to Him about these things.

DAY 16: DIG DEEPER

Read Genesis 22:1-19.

... and I got the strangest of answers to my prayer: *"Go to Jerusalem."* Once I understood this was not only an instruction but also an invitation, in just a few days I found myself in a budget Arab hotel on the Mount of Olives, within walking distance of the Old City. My one single view from the window was the magnificent Dome of the Rock on the Temple Mount.

My first outing into the Old City took me to the Pool of Bethesda where Jesus healed the man who had been lame for 38 years.[9] He questioned me as He had that man: *"Do you want to be well?"* My answer was *"Yes, Lord"*. The only water to be found on the site today was down very many steps to a pre-Roman level. At that point the Holy Spirit said to me: *"There IS living water but you will need to dig down deep into Me to find it"*. Dig down deep? Were there levels in me and depths in God that I had not yet reached? Absolutely! It seems I had stopped 'digging' and I needed to restart excavating my relationship with Him. From then on, my whole week was spent exploring underground Jerusalem, its ancient passages, tunnels and channels as the Lord hammered home the same message.

It was at the Western Wall of the Temple Mount that Father met with me personally. I had just finished praying the blessing of peace over Jerusalem (Psalm 122) when immediately I felt the Lord place His hand on my head and say: *"Peace I leave with you; My peace I give you. I do not give to you as the world gives. Do not let your heart be troubled and do not be afraid."*[10] He spoke peace into my spirit and I came home well and have remained so! Our English Bibles always translate the word shalom as 'peace'. But in

---

[9] John 5:1-13.
[10] John 14:27.

Hebrew it means much more e.g.: completeness, wholeness, health, peace, welfare, safety, soundness, tranquility, prosperity, perfectness, fullness, rest, harmony and the absence of agitation or discord. I prayed *shalom* over Jerusalem and He blessed *ME* with it instead! Through this experience I came to know God personally as my *Adonai Shalom* [Lord of Health & Wholeness]. Would I have received this healing without going to Jerusalem? Possibly, but when we hear God's Word, He expects us to obey it. It is not *knowing* the Word that digs the foundation of the house on the rock but *putting it into practice.*

It was only through obedience that God's covenant partner Abraham came to know Him as his provision. His encounter with God was on a rock; in fact, the very rock I looked out on from my Jerusalem bedroom window; the one covered today by the great Dome of the Rock, on the Temple Mount, a.k.a. Mount Moriah. As a result of my encounter on that *very same rock* I am different. Not only am I well, my foundation is stronger; I am more secure in the depth of His love towards me, deeper in love with Him and eager to keep on mining the depths of as-yet-untapped riches in Him. Tests since have proved the disease is 'incomplete' which I believe is medical-speak for God has healed me!

Additional reading: Psalm 107:28-30; John 16:33.

PRAYER TIME:

- *What does Jesus say about Himself in John 16:33?*

Ask Him to teach you how to dig in deeper in order to live as an overcomer.

DAY 17: EXCAVATIONS 1

Read 2 Corinthians 1:3-11.

Storms don't just go away; they are part of everyday life. God means us to so deepen our relationship in Him that we are able to live as overcomers *through* the storms and even reach out to others offering the real certainty and living hope of a relationship with God for themselves.

Over the next two days YOU are going to do some 'digging'!

PRAYER TIME:

Turn back to Day 13 Our Covenant Partner pp.34-35.

Read slowly through the 9 steps to covenant-making. As you do so, ask the Holy Spirit to highlight which of the 9 steps He wants you to focus on today. If you have time then perhaps consider doing more than one.

Prayerfully reflect on your chosen step. Consider the answers to the following questions:

- *What is this step teaching you about God's love and character?*
- *What is it showing you about how He sees you?*
- *What has He shown you about the value He places on your relationship with Him?*

Use a concordance or your favourite Bible programme or app to explore this aspect more. E.g.:

- *Can you find at least one scripture where this truth is reiterated somewhere else in the Old Testament?*

- *Can you find at least one scripture where this truth is restated by Jesus, Paul or one of the other writers?*

Write all your answers below:

DAY 18: EXCAVATIONS 2

Read 1 Corinthians 3:10-23.

The covenant blood of Jesus is our one true foundation. We are the carriers of His life to our world today but we must take great care what and how we build on His foundation. Anything other than following His ways will leave the 'building' open to the ravages of the elements.

Let us continue the 'digging'!

PRAYER TIME:

Turn back to Day 13 Our Covenant Partner pp.34-35.

Read slowly through the 9 steps to covenant-making. As you do so, ask the Holy Spirit to highlight which of the 9 steps He wants you to focus on today. If you have time then perhaps consider doing more than one.

Prayerfully reflect on your chosen step. Consider the answers to the following questions:

- *What is this step teaching you about God's love and character?*
- *What is it showing you about how He sees you?*
- *What has He shown you about the value He places on your relationship with Him?*

Use a concordance or your favourite Bible programme or app to explore this aspect more. E.g.:

- *Can you find at least one scripture where this truth is reiterated somewhere else in the Old Testament?*

- *Can you find at least one scripture where this truth is restated by Jesus, Paul or one of the other writers?*

Write all your answers below:

DAY 19: THE SPOIL

Read Ephesians 2:1-10; 1 Peter 1:13-16; 2:1-10; 2Peter 3:10-12;

Digging foundations - excavating - always produces a surplus of soil and stones that need to be removed from the site to allow the construction to go ahead. In some parts of the British Isles this excess hardcore is called 'spoil'. As we dig down deeper into our relationship with God, learning more of His character and the depth of His loving kindness and faithfulness towards us, we also see clearly that He is holy, just and right. The light of His holiness reflects onto us and exposes the things that spoil (blemish, ruin, destroy) our relationship. Today's readings show that God's desire is for us to be a holy (consecrated, set apart) people reflecting His character to others by the way we behave, so any spiritual hardcore needs to be removed. This 'spoil' falls largely into four areas:

1. *Fear and anxiety. This is particularly pertinent when we are dealing with personal storms that include people, finance, sickness and disease. Behind every fear is a lie of some kind we believe as truth.*
2. *Negative or destructive thoughts. These are also rooted in lies either about ourselves or about God.*
3. *Unforgiveness. We all get wounded by what others do or say, but holding onto unforgiveness only causes further hurt as we allow feelings of bitterness and resentment to take hold.*
4. *Sin and its resulting patterns of behaviour. We might use these as coping strategies to attempt to meet our legitimate needs for security, acceptance and significance through anyone or anything other than God.*

All of us have some degree of 'spoil' in our lives. We would be lying if we said we did not; however, as beloved children of our loving and patient covenant partner God, we no longer need to be bound by the limitations these things place upon us.

Additional reading: Leviticus 20:7; Psalm 27:1-5; Ephesians 4:17-32; Hebrews 12:15.

PRAYER TIME:

Look over the lists of 'spoil' above.

- *Ask the Holy Spirit to show you anything within each of the four areas where you know you do not trust Him with the outcome.*

Write them down.

Talk to God about these things. Ask Him to help you trust Him to be with you and on your side in whatever circumstances you face.

DAY 20: OCCUPYING...

Read Job 38; 1 Corinthians 6:19-20; 1 John 4:18-19.

The digging out of the spoil creates an empty space. If you look back to the original plan of Lundy's Old Light p.34 you will see that the foundation excavations resulted in a useful storage space. In spiritual terms, for us to proceed in being built into a spiritual lighthouse - a blazing stronghold of God's love, faith and hope - we need not only identify and dig out the 'spoil' but also make room for the Holy Spirit to come in and occupy the space that has been created in our hearts. Each of us is a sacred spiritual storage space (the Bible uses the word Temple) for the fulness of His love, life, energy, fruit and gifts. These are the very things which form the basis for His life being seen in and through us.

The way out is fivefold:

1. Gain a correct perspective of how big your covenant partner God is in comparison to your most prevalent storm (see Job 38).
2. Repent of not trusting Him e.g., giving into fear, unforgiveness, negative thoughts or sin. Be specific if you can.
3. Make the choice to believe that what the Bible says is true about His nature, character and His love towards you.
4. Resolve to live out your repentance through committing to godly choices. Ask for His help to keep strong in this resolve.
5. Deliberately invite Him to walk alongside you through your storm and make the choice to believe He will be with you.

Look back to the notes you made yesterday and sincerely work through the process outlined above for each 'spoil' listed. When you have finished, work through the following exercise of sincere consecration.

Additional reading Romans 6:12-14; Romans 12:1-2; 1 Peter 2:5.

PRAYER TIME:

A sacrifice is a gift or an offering made to God. The language Paul uses in these verses refers to the burnt offering in the Temple worship. The Hebrew word translated 'burnt' literally means 'that which arises or ascends.' When a burnt offering was given, everything was totally consumed on the altar; the body, carcass, blood, hair. In fact, the aroma was said to rise up and be pleasing to Father's nostrils!

In Romans 12:1 Paul implies we are the burnt offering. In the Old Testament it was the priests who made the offerings but Peter teaches that we are each part of the new priesthood, the body of believers. Therefore, the offering we are making today is ourselves – our whole lives.

Using Romans 6:13 and beginning with and from your mind and working down to your eyes, ears, mouth etc. take the time to intentionally offer your whole self and each individual part of your body to God for Him to use. Consciously set yourself apart to Him.

Take time to listen to Him concerning any direction He may have for you. Turn these thoughts into a prayer giving God permission to do everything He needs to do in you to make you the person He needs you to be to fulfil His plans in your life.

Ask the Holy Spirit to come in to fill you afresh today.

Ask Him to expand your faith, deepen your understanding of who God is and to pour His love into your heart in order for it to overflow out into the lives of others.

For more in-depth help and studies on the 'spoil' points please visit https://newbeginningsdiscipleship.wordpress.com/walking-with-god-in-relationship/

BUILDING
BEING SECURE IN GOD

It is time to begin construction. Ground Level is about bringing into the lighthouse stores everything that is needed so it can fulfil its purpose...

DAY 21: OUR CORNERSTONE

Read Isaiah 28:14-23; 1 Peter 2:4-9.

A lighthouse is constructed on a foundation dug right down to solid rock. If it were not so it could not stand the sheer strength of everyday waves and winds, let alone those of storm force. The necessity to repeatedly stand strong means that the first level of construction is of paramount importance; get ground level wrong and the whole thing could collapse at the first sign of trouble.

In a normal rectangular building, the cornerstone is the first stone laid at ground level from which every other measurement and alignment is made. In a circular construction like a lighthouse *every* stone is a key stone because measurements and alignments continue to be of paramount importance right to the very top of the building: should just one stone be out of true it would cause a weakness that could at some stage see the whole tower lean or collapse.

In Isaiah 28 God gives a grave rebuke to a nation that has installed shallow substitutes as their refuge and security and declares that He Himself will act in a 'stormy' judgement to sweep these things away. He makes it clear that He will lay a precious but tested cornerstone that will be the new plumbline for justice and righteousness in the nations. Scripture confirms Jesus - His life, suffering, blood, death and glorious resurrection - to be this cornerstone.

If we believe Jesus' blood to be the once for all defining sacrifice that sealed the New Covenant then this fact should be the cornerstone of our lives not just on the day we first acknowledge it but EVERY DAY. In the construction of the lighthouse, this foundational building block, measuring line and alignment is not to be just the starting block but the very essence, objective and certain hope of *everything* that is built, either deep within us or by us for His Kingdom.

Additional reading: Zechariah 10:4; Acts 4:11; Ephesians 2:20-22.

PRAYER TIME:

Reflect on what is written about the cornerstone and the difference between a rectangular and circular building.

- *Can you identify any parts within you or things you have done ostensibly for Him where you can see He was not the key-stone?*

Confess these things to God and receive His forgiveness.

Rededicate the 'cornerstone' of your spiritual building to God. Invite Jesus to help you build every layer of your life from hereon in with Him, His truth, righteousness and justice as your foundation, alignment and plumbline.

DAY 22: OUR STRONG TOWER

Read Psalm 46; Proverbs 18:2.

Early lighthouses were simply constructed stone on stone but this method quickly became a problem as structures easily crumbled when faced with severe storm lashings. A new way was developed using many layers of perfectly interlinked dovetailed stones which actually turned the lighthouse into a very strong tower. Speaking spiritually, unless the covenant blood of Jesus - in fact all that is found within the godhead and the written Word - is the dovetailed building block set in 'alignment' for every single aspect of our life from ground level to the very top what is built within us will not be able to stand strong in the face of storms. Jesus was a tested cornerstone so we too are tested; it is by living through the intensity of the very storms we face that we come to realise that maybe our relationship with God is not as deep or strong as we thought it to be...

In Psalm 46 the Psalmist describes a critical storm; every known point of reference is being shaken or destroyed and yet it is clear his confidence is in the imminent abiding presence of God. This was probably written when the Assyrian army surrounded Jerusalem[11] but it could equally be an analogy of how your life seems right now; it could even be a description of the state of the world immediately prior to Jesus' return.[12] What it describes is not the point because from verse 4 the author clearly directs us upwards, to take our attention away from the storm and to focus instead on God's throne-room. Even in the midst of pressing storms, the river of living water is still able to gladden our hearts, for we are set apart to be the place where the Spirit of the Most High dwells!!

---

[11] 2 Kings 18:13-19:37.
[12] Matthew 24.

The Psalmist does not pretend that the storm is not real but the declarations in verses 5-11 shows us his perspective is to choose to look to where God is. As his covenant partner, God will not let him or the people of God down. His heart-cry expressed in verse 10 is simply *"If the God you think you know isn't like this, then stop doing what you're doing and get to know Him...now..."*

Storms happen and our covenant God is on our side. His desire for us is for Him to be the very building blocks of every aspect of who He is within us and for us to be so secure in what that really means that when even greater storms hit, we will be able to stand strong and secure in Him, for Him.

Additional reading: Psalm 61.

PRAYER TIME:

On Day 1 we stated the lighthouse's over-riding purpose is to shine a light and sound a loud warning throughout the hours of darkness or the confusion of thick fog to prevent ships being wrecked and lives lost.

- *Can you think of any other roles the lighthouse might have?*
- *What does the image signify for you?*
- *Does the Lord's name 'Strong Tower' describe what you have written above?*

Spend time worshipping God for the wonder of who He is.

DAY 23: OUR REFUGE

Read Psalm 91.

Whenever I mention a lighthouse to someone, they usually mention the word 'refuge'. This is because we associate the light emitting from the lamp room with the warm glow and protection the lighthouse itself offers whereas actually the lighthouse's over-riding purpose is to send out the warning *'Do not come near here because there are dangerous rocks you need to avoid.'* So, it is understood that anyone reaching the sanctuary of the lighthouse will have first been through and overcome a rocky, challenging or stormy time.

A refuge can be many things e.g.: a shelter, a hiding place, a sanctuary or a safe place. It offers protection, safety, security or a temporary retreat from the pressures of the storm. It is a place of deep trust.

In Psalm 91 it is clear the Psalmist is strongly advising us to find our refuge in our relationship with our covenant partner God. As with all aspects of the covenant, receiving the blessings and living in them are conditional upon our obedience. So, if we expect God to step in and save us from the deadly pestilence, the plague, the fowler's snare and assist us in every battle and stormy situation but make no effort whatsoever to get to really know Him and to live in a way that pleases Him, then we are relying more on superstition rather than the purity of a covenant relationship.

God beckons us inside the shelter of the lighthouse to take refuge in Him. The offer is to firmly close the door on the distractions, fears and challenges of the stormy outside world and determine in our heart to shut ourselves in with God and to seize this opportunity to learn what it means to make Him our refuge.

PRAYER TIME:

Re-read Psalm 91 and note down the following:

- *The different names of God.*
- *What do these tell you about Him, His nature and how He sees you?*
- *Can you identify the responsibilities of both covenant parties?*
- *What must we do?*
- *What does God promise?*
- *What does He offer to those who make Him their refuge?*
- *How do we make Him our refuge?*
- *What is the key word in the whole Psalm (v.9)?*

Acknowledge your most prevalent storm to God and determine to trust Him with it.

Metaphorically close the door of your spiritual lighthouse making sure you leave the storm on the outside. From now on you are going to concentrate on building your relationship with God and not on the storm. Commit yourself to doing this now.

DAY 24: OUR FORTRESS

Read Psalm 62.

I live in the beautiful Eden Valley area of Cumbria and the landscape is littered with the ruins of a multitude of medieval castles, each one a testimony to our bloody and troubled past in the borderlands between the two nations of Scotland and England. Interestingly, in almost 100% of cases, even though the castle's outer walls may have fallen or been taken to build a local farmhouse, the Norman-built keep usually remains largely intact. Whilst a fortress is also a strong tower or refuge, the term 'fortress' strongly suggests a military stronghold, a keep or citadel; something that holds out resolutely against all outside influence or disturbance.

This is a tremendous picture of who God is: He is not only our covenant partner who has laid His entire spiritual armoury at our disposal (including myriads of the angelic host) but He is also actively supporting us through our storms and contending for us against all opposing spiritual assignments sent to knock us off course, sap our strength, bring discouragement or despair and consume our thoughts through every waking moment. God Himself is our complete protection - His presence, His covering, His shield of love in the blood of Jesus.

The even better news is that through the blood of Jesus we are recreated spiritually alive temples of the Spirit's presence. This is a complete game changer: we no longer have to accept being beaten down or overwhelmed by our storms because the indwelling Spirit can strengthen us so we too become built-up in Him to be a spiritual strong tower and fortress. The key is to welcome the Holy Spirit to make our heart His home, to make the choice to submit ourselves fully to God, maintain a humble heart that is willing to obey so then we can take heart and dare to believe that He will not only protect us and fight for us but strengthen us through the process. God is very much on our side; whilst it may seem we are facing our storms alone, that is a lie of the enemy. Our great covenant partner is with us and with Him alongside we will not be shaken by them.

Additional reading: Psalm 27:14; John 16:33; 2 Corinthians 5:17.

PRAYER TIME:

Re-read Psalm 62 and note down the following:

- *The different names of God.*
- *What do these tell you about Him, His nature and how He sees you?*
- *What impresses you most about the Psalmist's faith in God?*

Spend some time working through verse 8 for yourself. Pour your heart out to Him. Receive His peace.

DAY 25: OUR GOOD SHEPHERD

Read Psalm 23.

As I write, the new spring lambs are bouncing around in the field outside my kitchen window. They chase each other's tails, leap on top of one another, crawl under gates and fences and basically do their best to cause their mothers some heartache! I have lost count of the number of times we have to reunite a lost lamb with its stressed and baying mother. As non-farmers we get to observe the differences between shepherds. The careful and attentive shepherds visit most days, clip the feet of the lame and douse the fleeces before the maggots appear! Those not rated so highly are those who simply put the sheep in a field or hillside and neglect them for weeks at a time. Unsurprisingly these are the ones we usually have to ring to say we have found a dead sheep.

The role of shepherd is one of constant vigilance motivated by loving care and definitely includes a measure of sacrifice e.g.: getting up through the night to assist lambing mums, especially those with mal-presentations, being there to pick up an apparently dead lamb and fiercely rub or swing some life into it, being alert and aware of where the sheep are and the potential hazards they might encounter, where the predators might find their way in, is there enough grass or water and especially how many are there?

King David who wrote today's Psalm 23 was a shepherd in his youth. The whole Psalm describes his understanding of what it means to live in the security of a covenant relationship with God his Shepherd. He is totally assured that God's only thoughts towards him are for his good and well-being.

In verse 4 he acknowledges the inevitability of facing death (and David certainly faced death many times) but it is clear the strength of his awareness of God's constant presence meant there was no room in his heart for a foothold of fear. Deep within his heart David had built a stronghold of God's love, goodness and never-ending loving kindness towards him in which he was totally secure.

Additional reading: John 10:1-18.

PRAYER TIME:

Look back to Day 13 and the 9 steps to cutting a covenant.

- *Can you identify any of these stages in Psalm 23?*
- *If so, what does this say to you about God's character and nature?*
- *How does that affect how you see your own relationship with Him?*
- *Spend time meditating in prayer on verses 5 & 6 of Psalm 23.*

Consciously choose to give any areas of fear attached to your most prevalent storm to God. Repent of having given into this fear. Ask Him to fill your whole body afresh with the perfect love of His Spirit today. Rededicate your body as a spiritual temple, the house of Lord. May it be His dwelling place forever…

DAY 26: TOTALLY SECURE

Read Genesis chapters 2 & 3.

In the beginning God created us to have a very close relationship with Him where we would live knowing we are safe, secure, loved and cared for as well as having a real significance and purpose for life. But Adam and Eve blew it; they chose to live independently of Him. As their spiritual descendants we too have inherited a nature that pushes us to live independently of God, to take control. This is one of the reasons we have so much 'spoil' in our lives and wrestle with some self-induced storms.

We believe we know what is best for us so our pride urges us to try to rely on ourselves, our own instincts or the world's voice - ANYTHING other than God! We build our lives on a wrong foundation. Instead of exercising faith and believing what the Bible says about God is actually true, that He is our strong tower, refuge and fortress, we attempt to be strong in our own strength, provide for ourselves and fight our own battles our way. This strategy may have worked for us up until now but in the end, this will always be faulty; something built on sand which at some stormy point in the future will collapse.

The bottom line is we are ALREADY SECURE in Him. We need not be governed by guilt, shame and fear of being banished from His presence like Adam and Eve. We have a totally good, loving, caring, compassionate, protective, providing Father God who is constantly looking out for our well-being. Through the New Covenant in Jesus' blood, it is now possible for us to confidently approach Him for ourselves and He longs to be intimately involved in our everyday lives and for us to rely on Him to meet our basic needs for security, acceptance and significance instead of our trying to work out these things for ourselves. We just need to make the choice to believe it is true and trust Him. Psalm 62:8 reassures that we can trust in Him at all times. In fact, we can trust Him enough to pour out our hearts to Him for the one who is our covenant partner is also our rock, cornerstone, strong tower, refuge, fortress, strength, shield, salvation and very good shepherd.

Additional reading: Psalm 62; Hebrews 4:14-16.

PRAYER TIME:

Reflect on today's reading. Consider the HONEST answers to some of the following questions:

- *Who or what has been your security until now?*
- *Can you identify some of the reasons this is so important to you?*
- *In what way has this been a substitute for wholly trusting in God?*

Confess your failure to trust God in this area of your life and resolve to trust and to make Him your security from now on.

Talk to God about it all.

Please visit my website www.newbeginningsdiscipleship.wordpress.com. Scroll across to the Community tab then click on Community Resources. You will be able to download the music track *The Father Who Delights in You.*

Listen to this now. Take the time to allow this spoken truth to penetrate deep into your spirit.

ACCOMMODATION

KNOWING YOU ARE ACCEPTED BY GOD

The central section of the lighthouse provides the most secure shelter from the storm. It is completely protected on all sides and is therefore a safe place to rest, eat, sleep and be refreshed. The accommodation room is one open-plan space.

DAY 27: FRIENDS OF GOD

Read John 15:1-17; James 2:23.

I am one of those people who find it relatively easy to form new relationships and I am blessed to have people all over the world who I can call my friends. However, the truth is that the great majority are simply acquaintances, people I like and get on well with at a surface level but who do not really know me very well at all and vice versa. This modern familiarity is a long way removed from what the Bible terms 'friendship'.

Please look back to Day 13, the steps to covenant making. In step 9 becoming covenant friends was a very significant final stage of the bloody and solemn process. The declaration of friendship was only made once both parties fully understood their obligations and ongoing responsibilities and the final seal of the deal - the blood-sprinkled memorial tree - was firmly planted in the ground; only then, could we call one another friends.

Now that we have a greater understanding of whom our covenant partner is and feel secure in that, we too can begin to explore what it means to be called a 'friend of God' and live in the light of that every day. John 15:1-17 defines the terms of covenant friendship for us e.g.:

- *Verse 4 "Remain in Me, and I will remain in you."*
- *Verse 7 "If you remain in me and my words remain in you, ask whatever you wish, and it will be given you."*
- *Verses 13-14 "Greater love has no-one than this, that he lay down his life for his friends. You are my friends if you do what I command."*

In very simple terms, if we make every effort to remain (stay, continue, persist) in our relationship with God then we have the assurance that our covenant partner God will not only endure in His love, protection and provision for us but that we are accepted as His friend.

Additional reading: 2 Chronicles 20:7 Isaiah 41: 1-10.

PRAYER TIME:

- *What was it that made Abraham able to be called God's friend? There is more than one answer!!*

Re-read John 15:1-17. Make a note of every instance of covenant language used by Jesus.

- *What does this show you about the depth of your acceptance by God?*
- *Who is your covenant friend who laid down His life for you?*
- *What should be your response?*

DAY 28: LIVING TOGETHER

Read John 15:1-17; 1 Peter 4:1-11.

Living or sharing together does not necessarily come easily. I know several people who have gone on a much longed for holiday with their best friends only to return home with the relationship in tatters. Perhaps you have had guests or relations come to stay who insist on you adapting to *their* ways in *your* house, rather than the other way around?

What Jesus describes in John 15:1-17 is about us learning to live and share the whole of life with our covenant partner God. In verses 4-7 and 9-10 the N.I.V. uses the word 'remain' but I prefer the N.K.J.V. use of the word 'abide'. One definition of 'abide' is to live, settle down, inhabit or dwell together. Interestingly my English Thesaurus[13] defines abiding in more archaic terms: to 'abide' is to bear with, stomach, tolerate and put up with which explains why I have a memory of my grandmother saying in her West Country burr *"I can't abide that woman."* Putting the two meanings together we can see that when we live together, we also have to learn to tolerate and put up with one another and our various habits. For some of us this can be a storm in itself and involve us having to count to ten under our breath more than once in the day!

It is only by learning to trust and grow together in the relatively good times that we can support one another through the storms that inevitably come. This statement is also true of our relationship with God: His love is already enduring, faithful and unending towards us. When we are seeking to remain or abide in Him then it behoves us to consider some of the adjustments we might need to make in order to learn to live in a way that honours and pleases Him and that does not offend the presence of the

---

[13] Word 2013 online Thesaurus.

indwelling Holy Spirit. So, over the next few days we are going to spend time in the lighthouse 'accommodation' level and see what we can build into our way of life that pleases God's heart.

Additional reading: Psalm 55:8; Ecclesiastes 4:12; Amos 3:3.

PRAYER TIME:

Look back over today's readings.

- *Can you honestly say you feel accepted by God?*
- *What does having a friend like God mean to you?*

Write down what you think might be required for you to be built stronger in your relationship with Him.

- *Why have you singled out those things?*

Talk to the Lord about all these things. Thank Him that He has accepted you and for being your true friend.

DAY 29: FELLOWSHIP WITH GOD

Read Genesis 3:8; Exodus 19:1-9.

Fellowship is one of those overused and much misunderstood words within the church today. There is a great spectrum of interpretation between having a mild affiliation, rather like belonging to a secular club or society, right through to those who have a thorough grasp of being co-workers in the serious matter of the gospel. We might spend 30 years sharing a cup of tea after a morning service with members of a congregation and still not experience any true fellowship or we could have a deeply meaningful level after chatting with someone for just five minutes! This unique spiritual bond comes from a family bloodline through our shared relationship in Jesus. Without us knowing how or why the Holy Spirit connects us spirit to spirit with other family members. This supernatural bond will become vitally important as the greater spiritual storm over the whole world increases and the days get darker.

In the beginning God created Adam and Eve to have unrestricted fellowship with Him. He was actively involved in their everyday existence so they knew what it was to feel totally secure, loved and accepted, to belong to God. Yet they rejected Him. Exodus 19 relates how God brought the Hebrews out of Egypt not only to free them from slavery but to bring them to Himself, so they might enjoy the potential of that intimate relationship He had once enjoyed with Adam and Eve.

Clearly fellowship[14] - real deep mutual abiding companionship and friendship - between God and us is the spirit of covenant relationship and is therefore a priority on His heart. This should not be something forced or artificial and it definitely does not have to be ritualistic; God simply wants

---

[14] Strong's 2842 *koinonia* fellowship, partnership, contribution, participation and sharing.

to be an active participant and contributor in our lives, sharing and being involved in our everyday rather than a remote observer. True friends simply love each other, confide and share intimacies and give one another special time. They do things just to bless the other party and learn that friendship grows when we give as well as take! When these elements are present on both sides, not just one, then we have a level of unconditional acceptance and a true bond of fellowship.

Additional reading: John 14:23; 2 Corinthians 13:14.

PRAYER TIME:

Reflect on today's reading.

- *Is God an active participant in your everyday life or do you keep Him at arm's length in some way?*
- *If so, what needs to change in you to allow your relationship and fellowship to deepen and mature?*

Spend some conscious fellowship time with God: share your day, your problems, questions, doubts and storms with Him.

Meditate on the wonder of John 14:23 then thank Him for His fellowship.

DAY 30: INTIMACY WITH GOD

Read Psalm 23; Psalm 42; 1 John 4:18.

In modern society intimacy is a word commonly associated with a sexual relationship but actually this is a misrepresentation of its true meaning. We find true intimacy when the mutual bond of friendship is so easy, close and undemanding that we can exist for hours without having to do or say anything that disrupts the warmth and peace of the place of rest.

In Psalm 23, especially verses 2-3, it is clear David has found a dwelling place of the abiding presence of God deep within his heart that is not only peaceful but also restores and refreshes his very soul. There is no room for striving, worry, fear or trying to work it out, only tender quiet, almost bold confidence, in the ability of his covenant Shepherd (who he knows will never let him down or leave him to face storms alone) to guide him through. Once this intimacy is reached in our relationship with God we need never fear again because we have understood the nature of true covenant love completely.

If only we could stay in this idyllic state metaphorically gliding about a metre off the floor!! The problem is that the storms of everyday life, especially the people and problems we face, mean it is nigh-on impossible for us to maintain living in this perfect place of rest and peace. It is from this point another psalmist wrote Psalm 42. He does not pretend the storm in his heart is not present but he also knows his only way out - the only path to inner peace and rest - is for him to look upwards and invest in making time to meet with God. In fact, from the language used in verses 1 & 2 every fibre of his spirit cries out with longing, passion and desire for God. In verses 5 & 11 he addresses himself as if to stir up his spirit to seek God again.

One of the keys to standing strong through our storms is through nurturing the desire to truly dwell (stay, reside, inhabit, lodge[15]) moment by moment in His presence. It is in this place of restful intimacy God begins to build the abiding assurances of His love, faithfulness and certain hope deep within us.

Additional reading: Psalm 84; 1 Corinthians 13:13.

PRAYER TIME:

- *How do you meet with God?*
- *Would you describe this meeting as limited to a certain time slot or are you aware of God with you throughout your day?*
- *Are you satisfied with the level of spiritual intimacy you have with God?*
- *If not, then what steps will you take?*

Invite the Holy Spirit to come and walk with you throughout the whole of your day.

---

[15] Word 2013 online Thesaurus.

DAY 31: PURITY FOR GOD

Psalm 119:1-16; Hebrews 10:19-25.

Let us be honest; no-one likes living in close proximity with someone who does not wash regularly or smells! It is simply unpleasant and in today's world, unnecessary. True covenant friendship means we will do whatever it takes to please the other party and stay in the intimacy of fellowship so it should be obvious that at all times we need to aim for cleanliness and purity in our walk with God.

Spiritual uncleanness causes a barrier because we automatically withdraw to what we consider to be a safe distance! Let us be clear about this; it is not God who does the withdrawing, it is us. I know when I have left the place of intimacy because I no longer feel the Spirit's closeness and I struggle to hear His voice. Like Adam and Eve, I try to hide and cover up, until the light bulb moment where I wake up and realise I am truly missing His fellowship. There is a way back; it is through confession, repentance and a fresh sincere re-consecration.

Whilst we live and breathe, we will continue to clumsily say things that hurt or offend or find temptation overwhelm us with its resulting mess. We will not be completely wholly sanctified (set apart to God) until the day we die and receive our new spiritual body. We should not allow these struggles to become a barrier which will prevent us from pressing deeper into building our relationship with God. He accepts us as we are but in order to gain a deeper level of fellowship and intimacy we cannot stay as we are. He uses His Word - whether spoken, written or intuitive - but inspired by the Holy Spirit to illuminate the areas in our heart where He is still not Lord.

The Psalmist in today's reading understands our dilemma. How can we stay pure? By obeying God's Word. How do we know what His Word says? We read, study, meditate and memorize it. It is the very Word of God, inspired by the Spirit's power that gives us the desire to be different, leads us to repentance and assures us of our renewal and restoration.

Additional reading: 1 Corinthians 6:9-11; 2 Timothy 3:16-17; Hebrews 4:12.

PRAYER TIME:

- *How do you study God's Word?*
- *Do you ever take time to meditate or marinade a scripture in your Spirit throughout the day?*

Commit today's verse Hebrews 4:12 to memory.

Take time to meditate on the different characteristics of God's voice outlined in the verse.

- *Consider your life: what is God saying to you?*

Write down what you hear.

Thank God that when He looks at you, He sees you washed, clean and made holy through the New Covenant in Jesus blood.

DAY 32: FEEDING ON GOD

Read Psalm 119:89-112; Isaiah 11:1-3.

When we spend quality time with someone conversation happens. Of course, there are long times of companionable silence but we also talk. If we do not then perhaps there is an issue to be addressed! The important thing about conversation is that it should be a two-sided dialogue - an exchange of words, thoughts and concepts - not just a one-sided monologue! When we translate this into our relationship with God and especially our prayer lives, we can be guilty of assaulting God's ears with long lists of our needs and reminding Him of situations He is already aware of! That is not wrong, but sometimes we just need to stop chattering, be quiet and pay Him the honour of LISTENING to what He might have to say. Isaiah writes that God's Spirit gives us heavenly wisdom, understanding, counsel and insight; it also empowers and strengthens. So why would we not take time to listen to Him?

Ideally our daily conversation and refreshment time with God should include the basic minimum of worship, prayer and some form of study in the Bible.

We are different people and we all feed on Him differently: some need visual stimulation so spend hours watching sermons on YouTube (!) whereas others only read and truly soak in studying the Bible for themselves, with or without daily Bible reading aids; others simply tarry (linger, stay, wait) in His presence throughout the whole day alert for when He speaks and what He has to say. My first priority each day is to engage in heart-to-heart worship (not just listening to songs) during which my whole focus is on God. From that place of intimate fellowship, I alert my spirit to listen for what God has to whisper back to me and I simply wait. His Word may come in several forms: a scripture or text to look up and read that may stay with me throughout the day as the Holy Spirit marinades it in my spirit, a picture that sheds light on an issue or guides me forward, a burning conviction that I have either done or said something wrong that must be confessed and put right or something I must do immediately e.g., call or visit someone to make sure they are o.k... When writing this devotional, the Lord invariably downloaded the next day's content whilst I was asleep at night!! So, there are many different ways in which God speaks. Generally, these will concern the following areas: our relationship with Him, to guide us in His will and His ways, to help strengthen us through our storms and meet our needs, to change our character or learn obedience or to allow us to speak into someone else's situation.

Additional reading: Psalm 34:1-10.

PRAYER TIME:

- *How do you 'feed' on the Lord and find your spiritual refreshment?*
- *How do you usually hear God's voice?*
- *How do you know it is God's voice and not some other thought or imagination?*

Spend some time quietly waiting on God. Ask Him to speak to you.

OPERATIONS
KNOWING YOUR SIGNIFICANCE TO GOD

The top-most level of the lighthouse is the place of work: it is where the keeper of the light keeps the watch and tends the flame of the lamp.

DAY 33: SIGNIFICANT PURPOSE

Read John 8:12; Matthew 5:14-16.

Most lighthouses today are unmanned and fully automated. The Old Light on Lundy was built in 1819 when the lamp that shone from the lamp platform was fuelled by oil and the keepers took turns in working 24 hours 7 days a week 365 days a year to do everything possible to keep the lamp burning. In addition to this they lived in a constant state of vigilance as they kept the watch to look out for those in danger. There was a whole team of people willing to risk their lives to put out tiny rowing boats from the shore to sail headlong into danger to rescue those in trouble through storms.

Spiritually speaking Jesus is the very essence of every single living stone out of which the whole spiritual lighthouse is built: from the depths of the bedrock, the foundations, the cornerstone from which all alignments are made, through every level of construction right to the very top. The Spirit of God is even the oil that gives light to the lamp and He Himself is the Light. We are significant people who have been called and chosen to have the same commission the light-keepers once had: to maintain and shine the light, keep the watch and do everything humanly possible to put out the spiritual lifeboat to save and rescue those who are caught up in a storm - whether that be spiritually, physically, mentally or emotionally.

It is only from the place of solid foundation of our understanding of covenant relationship with God and embracing what that means for us, that we are enabled to put our own storms into perspective. Then from a place of security and acceptance in Him, offer out to others the arm of certain hope that is found in a relationship with God through Jesus.

Additional reading: 2 Corinthians 4:6; Hebrews 6:13-19.

PRAYER TIME:

Think about the spiritual interpretation of the 'operations' level of the lighthouse. Ask the Holy Spirit to show you what this might mean for you and your walk with God.

- *What is your spiritual purpose?*

Write down what He says.

Ask Him to kindle His Light within you that you might burn even stronger than before.

DAY 34: THE LIGHT OF LIFE

Read John 8:12; 10:10; Ephesians 1:15-23; 1 Peter 2:9.

When we learn to follow Jesus, we possess and enjoy the Light of Life. This speaks of every single aspect of vibrant spiritual life that flows to us through the covenant blood of Jesus.

One of the special attributes of blood is the way it circulates throughout the whole body delivering essential substances like oxygen and nutrients to the body's cells. It also transports waste products away from those same cells. There is no substitute for blood. It cannot be made or manufactured; it alone is responsible for carrying the message of life to every vital organ, muscle, cell and minute tendril of body tissue. Without our blood we would be dead. Essentially this is the message of the Cross: without the covenant blood of Jesus, we are dead in our sins, living under a veil of spiritual darkness which covers our thoughts, emotions, choices, behaviour and all other parts of our body, inside and out. Meeting Jesus changes everything: just like turning on the light in a darkened room suddenly illuminates the whole atmosphere, when we see Jesus our spiritual eyes perceive Him clearly as genuine Truth; the darkness in our hearts is exposed for what it is and dispersed.

Many believers stay at the Cross and never grow beyond understanding their personal salvation but truly there is more. There is also a whole host of life-giving and enhancing spiritual equivalents of oxygen, nutrients and proteins that are freely given to us through the blood of Jesus: we are not only covenant friends with God but also heirs of a great spiritual inheritance that, when understood, gives us the potential to live an abundant supernatural life. 'Abundance' speaks of a profusion of fruit, so once we gain a grasp of just how great a change the blood of Jesus has bought for us, we will truly glow from the inside out with Spirit-fuelled joy and peace which are the outward signs that we are carriers of the Light of Life.

Additional reading: Romans 15:13; Ephesians 2:10.

PRAYER TIME:

Ephesians 2:10. The word translated 'workmanship' implies we are akin to a work by a great artist that is put on display so that those who see it can admire the painter or sculptor's skill and handiwork. Meditate on this.

- *What does this say to you about how God sees you?*

If you have not already listened to the track *The Father Who Delights in You* on my website www.newbeginningsdiscipleship.wordpress.com then please do so today. On the website scroll across to the Community tab, then click the link to Community Resources. You will be able to download the music track.

Listen to this now. Take the time to allow this spoken truth to penetrate deep into your spirit.

- *Is the Holy Spirit highlighting any particular truth to you?*

Ask Him what He wants you to learn from this.

DAY 35: THE OIL

Read Exodus 27:20-21; Isaiah 11:1-3; Zechariah 4:6.

The most important task for the Victorian light-keeper was to keep the lamp constantly supplied with oil, otherwise it simply could not burn. We have a picture of this in the ministry of Aaron and the Levites within the Tabernacle. The lamp they tended was the seven-branched Menorah which is often referred to as a candlestick. This is a misnomer because it was actually a massive oil lamp whose light illuminated the whole Tabernacle structure.[16]. The oil used was pure; pressed from crushed olives. Isaiah's prophetic description of the Menorah in 11:1-3 confirms this to have been a complete foreshadowing of Jesus Messiah (the Branch from Jesse) and the 7-fold anointing of the 'Spirit of the Sovereign Lord' that rested on Him. He was able to shine and make a difference as the Light of the World because of the extent to which He was covered and bathed, in the glory of the Holy Spirit's oil. Wherever He went He not only carried the light but was Himself the true Light of Life. His spirit was 'crushed' in Gethsemane yet the pure 'oil' that flowed from His sacrifice truly brought the Light of Life to the whole world.

The Tabernacle was an earthly representation of God's home with His people. It was a constant reminder to them of the light of His presence, holiness, protection and fellowship. The priests were instructed to keep watch over the lamps because if the oil dried up and the light went out the Tabernacle would have been overwhelmed by darkness - the complete antithesis of God's intention. SO, every effort had to be made to keep the

---

[16] . Every single aspect of the Menorah represents the fulfilment of the covenant in Jesus Messiah and the seven Biblical Feasts. For more information on the feasts please see *Biblical Feasts*
https://newbeginningsdiscipleship.wordpress.com/shop/

oil in the lamp and the light from the fires in the seven sconces burning. Zechariah understood that unless there is a constant supply of spiritual oil, everything we do, all our efforts are done in human strength and are therefore merely good works. Anything of lasting value for God's Kingdom needs to flow from the Source of all life by the Spirit of God. So, we need to ensure we tend our spiritual lamps by constantly spending time in His presence being filled and refilled with His holy oil.

Additional reading: Matthew 25: 1-13; Luke 4:18-19.

PRAYER TIME:

Consider the importance of the anointing of the Holy Spirit in Jesus' ministry.

- *What does this teach us about its significance for us too?*
- *Does your understanding of spiritual oil shed light on the meaning of the oil in the virgins' lamps; those that had it and those that did not?*
- *Can you make a link with Zechariah 4:6?*

Give the remainder of your time today to fellowship time with God.

DAY 36: ENCROACHING DARKNESS

Read Matthew 24:9-25; 2 Timothy 3:12.

The Special Air Service (S.A.S.) is an elite force unit of the British Army. It was founded in 1941 to undertake a number of roles including underground reconnaissance, counter-terrorism, direct action and hostage rescue. Members of the S.A.S. are highly trained individuals who appear to be utterly fearless and therefore also feared by their enemies. One of the reasons they can operate to this standard is that they are utterly set apart inwardly to the tasks they are called to undertake.

The role of the S.A.S. is something very akin to that of the early church. In Acts we read of the severe persecution of the believers by Paul prior to his encounter with Jesus.[17] Persecution did not end with Paul's conversion; it increased to such an extent that all of the apostles were either imprisoned, martyred or both and this level of suffering and oppression continued until the 'conversion' of Constantine the Great around 313AD.

For almost 130 years (1532 - 1660[18]) England experienced extreme religious persecution: Protestants persecuted Catholics then Catholics turned the tables and hunted down Protestants with this reversal happening not once but several times. I understand that around 1650 the first minister of one Baptist Church in Bristol was tarred, feathered then tied to a cart before being dragged to where he was hung, drawn and quartered! It was not for nothing that the early Baptists - many of whom endured severe persecution and martyrdom - were called 'Radical Believers'. They knew their God and He knew them; just like the modern S.A.S. they were not

---

[17] Acts 22:4-7.
[18] From Henry VIII's break with Rome to the end of Cromwell's Commonwealth.

afraid to defend their cause. They were an underground church, meeting in homes, barns and outside spaces; they provided safe houses and refuge but above all they remained resolute in their faith: they preached the Word, baptised converts (in mill ponds and streams) and taught new believers to obey God over and above anything or anyone else. I often pray that God would put their D.N.A. in me...

Additional reading: Psalm 119:161-162; Mathew 5:10-12; Revelation 12:10-17.

PRAYER TIME:

Reflect on all you have read today. None of us warm to the notion of being persecuted but slowly and subtly our religious freedoms are already being eroded. Write down any ways in which you feel silenced or constrained from sharing your faith.

- *Why do you feel this way?*

Look back to Day 13 and remind yourself how great your covenant partner God is. Talk to Him about your fears and doubts. Listen to what He says to you.

DAY 37: WATCH, LISTEN, WARN

Read Luke 12.

Whilst it is comforting to think of a lighthouse as somewhere warm and safe, a snug shelter from the elements (and this is true!) we must not lose sight of its primary purpose which is to send out a warning of dangerous rocks and impending loss of life. Speaking spiritually this is our job too. We are not only called to shine the Light of Life but to station ourselves at our spiritual watch. This speaks of the prayer room: we not only need to give time to fellowship with God but we also need to be willing to sit humbly in His presence waiting for Him to speak and with a heart to obey actively listening to what He has to say to us. As the darkness encroaches and it becomes more difficult for believers to gather together with the ease we have known, hearing directly from God for ourselves will become of paramount importance. If we can maintain a level of personal intimacy with God then He will not only give us wisdom about where to go and what to do but also increase our spiritual discernment about who we are to share the things we are hearing with. This will be a vital commodity for us to live as overcomers and fulfill our purpose in the days ahead.

Sometimes we may have to share, test and weigh what we have heard amongst the wider Body of Christ for in truth we are not one isolated lighthouse but a whole group aiming to stand tall and strong for God in the same stormy sea. Back in 2008 our regional prayer team received a strong prophetic word in which God gave a powerful warning of dark stormy days ahead for the world and the church. The challenge was for us to prepare our hearts, our homes and the people of God. The Holy Spirit so convicted us with a sense of urgency and responsibility for sharing this message that for three months a friend and I travelled throughout the country sharing it and I continued to do so into the following year. We are now beginning to walk through the very situations the Lord warned us to prepare for...

Additional reading: Habakkuk 2:1; Luke 20:20; Acts 20:28.

PRAYER TIME:

Consider a world where persecution is more obvious and evil.

- *Why might it not be wise to use the internet, smart phones and social media at that time?*

Think beyond yourself to your social network too…

- *What might be the implications of your using social media for them?*

During the COVID-19 outbreak of 2020 I was literally inundated with contacts sending me various You Tube clips or Bible teachings which were mainly conspiracy theory based. I quickly reached saturation point!

- *Who should we really be taking time to listen to?*
- *Why is that?*
- *How do you hear from God?*
- *Do you believe He speaks to you?*

Ask Him to build your confidence to believe what He says to you and to give you someone you trust with whom you can share and weigh what you are hearing.

Ask Him to give you boldness to share His warnings sensitively.

DAY 38: STRONG IN HIM

Read Colossians 1:9-14; Ephesians 3:14-21; Revelation 19:11-21.

When we enter the Kingdom of God we do so from the territory of an opposing kingdom of darkness. The Bible clearly indicates that Satan is our chief enemy and his is the spirit that drives the world's end-time agenda. God's Word stands as a written testimony that these things must happen before Jesus returns. The Spirit warns us and testifies to our spirits that these things are true. Whilst the enemy will throw every storm in his armoury at us to discourage, disappoint, defeat and prevent the church being effective in God's service, he is actually a defeated foe and terrified of the children of God who know who their God truly is and, as a result, also know their immense worth and significance to Him.

The journey of the past six weeks has been allowing God to form a stronghold of His love, faith and certain hope deep inside:

- *The covenant love of God is our bedrock.*
- *We apply this through faith in the blood of Jesus.*
- *God is thoroughly for us and on our side; we are secure.*
- *He totally loves us and longs for us to reciprocate by learning to live every day in the intimacy and companionship of relationship; we are accepted.*
- *Our purpose is to let the Light of Life within pierce the darkness in the environs around us giving testimony and glory to what God has done in us; we are significant.*

Revelation 19:11-21 gives a description of an end-time army riding out behind their leader Jesus as He finally overcomes the beast. Whilst this refers to a time still a whole way off in the future nevertheless, we are already being prepared to ride out with Him. Knowing our security, acceptance and significance in God's covenant love are the essence of the true elite force - the spiritual S.A.S.[19] When we really begin to comprehend this we can *"...grasp how wide and long and high and deep is the love of Christ..."*. Then we will be able *"...to know this love that surpasses knowledge."* As we reach out in faith and drink these truths deep into our spirits then we *"...may be filled [with the oil of the Spirit] to the measure of all the fullness of God."* At this point, the enemy is more scared of us than we are of him. Each of us has the potential to be as highly trained and useful a spiritual unit for God's Kingdom as the Army's S.A.S.!

Additional reading: Ephesians 6:10-19.

PRAYER TIME:

Reflect on the journey of these notes.

- *What has God taught you about His love and character?*
- *What has He shown you about how He sees you?*
- *What has God shown you about the value He places on your relationship with Him?*
- *How have you grown in your relationship with Him?*

Spend the remainder of your time today in the oil room of worship, prayer and listening.

_____

[19] Security = S. Acceptance = A. Significance = S.

THE LAMP ROOM

BURNING FOR GOD

*The final level of the lighthouse is the lamp room itself;
the place where the fire burns.*

DAY 39: CHANGED PERSPECTIVE

Read Deuteronomy 28:13; Ephesians 1:19-23; 2:6-7.

Returning to Lundy's Old Light, we are made aware of the light from the lamp room even before we finish ascending the final staircase. After the almost complete darkness and stone coldness of the lighthouse interior the tantalising glimpse of warm bright sunlight compels us to keep climbing upwards. Suddenly we find ourselves brought out into a spacious place with a completely different atmosphere. In reality we cannot walk on anything but a narrow gangway around the perimeter of the massive platform where the lamp would once have sat but nevertheless it feels light, bright, airy and roomy. The 360° view is totally absorbing as it is not only possible to see the land and sea immediately below but also beyond that to the island's extremes and then on to the coasts of South Wales, Cornwall, Devon and the Bristol Channel. The perspective has opened up; it is completely different.

Speaking spiritually this echoes the journey we have taken over the past six weeks together: we are no longer slaves to fear, locked in at ground level to the limitations of our most prevalent storms because by gaining a greater understanding of our covenant relationship with God we have been enabled to put these into an entirely different perspective. In Ephesians 1:20-23 Paul teaches that when Jesus was raised from the dead God raised Him up over every ruling power and placed EVERYTHING under His feet. He goes on in chapter 2 verse 6 to say that because we are 'in Christ' God has also raised us up and seated us in heavenly places with Him. He is with us and on our side. Therefore, why would we fear?

The lamp room at the very top of the lighthouse literally shakes with the buffeting from strong winds. Sometimes the rain lashes on the panes so strongly it would not be surprising if it came right through! We all have to face storms; we cannot just push a button for them to go away and sometimes they are simply so strong we feel almost overwhelmed day after day. From our new understanding of our covenant relationship through Jesus' blood we genuinely have the ability to live as overcomers - to be the head and not the tail. We learn to put our storms into perspective i.e., look for the bigger picture of what God might be doing or wanting us to learn, to submit our desire to revert to learned patterns of behaviour or coping mechanisms and call on Him to be alongside to help or fight for us. If we walk with Him, we will have peace. The choice is ours.

Additional reading: Psalm 31:7-8; Psalm 118:1-8.

PRAYER TIME:

Look back to the most prevalent storm you identified on Day 2.

- *How has your perspective on this storm changed?*
- *How have you changed?*
- *How has your perspective of God changed?*

Spend time in worship and praise. Thank God for enlarging your perspective on who He is and enabling you to put your storms into context.

DAY 40: SHINING LIKE STARS!

Read Isaiah 30:26; Philippians 2:12-18; 1 Peter 2:9; Revelation 12:11.

I am privileged to live in a dark sky area where, because of the absence of all artificial street-lighting, the night sky itself can be enjoyed. I have lost count of the number of nights I have simply stood and looked heavenward, overawed by the magnificent splendour of the stars and their constellations. If they were not there our night time world would not only be completely dark but we would miss the testimony to their Creator their presence shouts aloud.

The promise of Jesus is that those who walk with Him [in covenant relationship] will have or carry the Light of Life.[20] Our purpose is to let that light shine in the darkness. When our lamps are constantly being replenished with spiritual oil then our witness to the goodness and love of God should see us standing out boldly for God in our ungodly nation in the same way the stars stand out against the dark night sky.

There is a sense of encroaching spiritual darkness over the whole world. None of us can know with certainty what lies ahead. The only cert is that we are called to be people whose presence makes a difference. Peter writes *"...to declare the praises of Him who called you out of darkness..."* so that others can see it and find Him for themselves. Never before in the whole of human history has the challenge for God's Spirit-filled people to testify been so great.

All prophetic scripture is multi-layered and may carry an interpretation for more than one era in time. One interpretation of Isaiah 30 and especially v26 is for the end-times. It depicts how God's children have an abundance of His favour, provision and anointing whilst the rest of the earth is reeling,

---

[20] John 8:12.

suffering judgment and affliction. The reference to seven full days is a picture of the Menorah (the fullness of Christ overflowing with the fullness of the Spirit) that will give a light like that of the sun but up to seven times brighter than ever before. Imagine - even seven times brighter than Pentecost as described in Acts 2! This is the context for which we are being prepared: it will be very dark but the Light of Life we carry will be far greater and have authentic power to overcome. The church will be busy saving lives; preaching will be bolder; healings will be commonplace and set free captives will turn society upside down!

Additional reading: 2 Corinthians 4:4-6; Ephesians 2:10.

PRAYER TIME:

- *What is your reaction to today's challenge?*
- *What are your fears and/or concerns?*
- *Are you afraid you will let God down?*
- *Can you identify any particular 'good work' you sense God might have prepared in advance for you to do?*

Spend time in worship, listening and sharing with your loving covenant partner. Tell Him all your doubts and fears. He understands. He also promises never to leave you or forsake you...

DAY 41: MAGNIFY HIS NAME

Read Psalm 96; Acts 5:1-11.

On Day 1 I related the story of how my friend and I witnessed the tiny lights from two small candles placed on the lamp platform of Lundy's Old Light miraculously magnified thousands of times until we could no longer count the number of lights. Put simply, our job is to do what the lenses, mirrors and the glass do in the lighthouse which is to reflect and magnify (enlarge or expand) the glorious Name of our covenant-keeping God. We do this by how we act, what we say and what we do.

We might think that having reached the pinnacle of the lighthouse there is absolutely no way we could do anything other than glorify His Name but actually our flesh nature often causes us to keep back something for ourselves. This is exactly what happened with Ananias and Sapphira. Despite their outward 'godly' appearance and seemingly generous giving, their motive was faulty. Not only did they keep back something financial, they also kept back a part of their heart. Whilst projecting the outward appearance of being as 'on fire' for God as their contempories, in their hearts they wanted to steal God's glory. They wanted to be highly spoken of and admired, seen to be someone and to have a reputation as generous givers. It was all a lie and their hearts were far from God. Judgement was swift and clear cut.

Back in 2006 when our ministry and influence was beginning to spread, I was being offered opportunities to speak from large well-known Christian platforms and the allure of this world was very tempting because I was beginning to be known and make a name for myself. Then one day God used an old woman I had never seen before or since to speak the truth into my heart. She prophesied that if I allowed myself to carry on using these open doors to build my own reputation then I would seriously displease and dishonour my God who I thought I was pleasing!! She did not do this privately; she said it to me in a crowded room where I was leading the meeting!!! I collapsed that day, pride deflating like a pierced balloon. Having learnt this painful and humbling lesson I am now content to stay low-key, in the background, trying to just meekly follow where He leads, only walking through the doors He opens and trying at all times to only do what He wants me to do.

Even when we know the truth about who He has called us to be in Him, we need to ensure that the Light of Life we carry remains pure and glorifies no other name than the Name of Jesus, for God does not share His glory with anyone. Any other light simply does not have the power to overcome the darkness for the simple reason elements of darkness are still present in it.

Additional reading: Psalm 86:11; Isaiah 42:8; John 3:19.

PRAYER TIME:

Reflect on today's reading.

- *Have you ever thought you were serving God but were actually guilty of serving yourself as well?*

Repent of the things He has shown you. Ask Him to give you a humble undivided heart.

Give the rest of your time today to magnifying Him using Psalm 96.

DAY 42: THE OLD WAY

Read Jeremiah 6:16; Isaiah 46:9-13; Revelation 1:4-8.

None of us knows what storms lie ahead. Life can be good one minute and suddenly it changes. When I was on Lundy in October 2019, the weather was balmy and warm. It was the calm before the storm. The Lord told me that before long I would be walking a more isolated and difficult path, one in which I would have to dig deeper into my relationship with Him because there would not be anyone else to rely on. This has become true during Coronavirus lockdown but I sense there is still a much harder path ahead for us all. The morning I left the island a storm suddenly hit land with ferocious violence. Our sailing had to be brought forward and diverted to a nearer harbour for safety's sake.

Just as in the days of Jeremiah our nation and the world stand at a crossroads. We have drifted so far away from God's Word and His standards that the choice is stark: either turn back or face judgement. Jeremiah addressed an Israel who had resolutely not turned and who were therefore suffering the ignominy of 70-years' exile in Babylon. We also face an uncertain future as God works out His end-time purposes to finally overthrow the spirit of Babylon and bring, not just Britain but, all the nations of the world into relationship with Him. What many of us fail to realise is this: that which was on God's heart for His relationship with us way back as far as the Garden of Eden, is still on His heart today. He is the Alpha and the Omega, the beginning and the end, the One who does not and never will change and whose purposes from the very beginning will stand. The ancient way of walking with Him is the same way Abraham, Moses, David and Jesus walked. It is the way of covenant relationship He has ordained and has now provided for us in Jesus' blood.

One day during the imposed lockdown of the Coronavirus epidemic I went for my permitted daily walk. The sun was warm and the afternoon was glorious so I walked high onto the disused railway along the head of the Eden Valley where I have lived for 22 years. I sat down close to the summit and suddenly my mind was filled with the wonder of God's enduring covenant love and His heart for relationship with us, yearning right back as far as the Garden from which our valley takes its name. He has always longed for a people who would walk with Him day by day in simple humble, meek, obedience, friendship, fellowship and companionship. My heart began to race as I poured out to God pure worship - the overflow of a deep, deep gratitude - for His faithfulness, especially in His provision of His only Son Jesus so that I could have the possibility of living and walking in this relationship myself. As my heart burned, I realised He had rekindled within me a flame of passion for Him and the things of God I had allowed to grow dim. At that moment of submission and refilling with the Spirit's oil I clearly heard the voice of God say

"This is the lesson I brought you to the Eden Valley to learn. It's all been about this - to walk with Me. Seek My face and glorify only My Name, then My covenant Light - the true 'Old Light' from Eden - will truly shine and be seen in you."

This is the very simple ancient way. It is the way of peace and rest.

Additional reading: Exodus 33:12-22; Isaiah 60:1-3.

You are now very close to the spiritual place near God where you may stand on a rock [the Rock] and see His glory pass by.

Imagine standing on the lamp platform at the top of the lighthouse and declare His goodness into the spiritual atmosphere over your life. Rededicate yourself completely - heart, mind, emotions, will and physical body - to God. Invite Him to fill you afresh with His holy oil and so to set your heart on fire so you can 'burn' for Him.

POSTSCRIPT
CARRYING THE 'OLD LIGHT'

In the winter of 2004, I was seeking a holiday cottage in Cornwall where I could go for a few days to simply spend some time with God. My search was frustrated at every turn. It was only when I stopped to pray the Lord suddenly put Lundy Island into my spirit. So began my long fascination with Lundy's Old Light.

At that time, I could never have imagined the rich spiritual journey I was about to embark on and the profound lessons I would eventually learn ...

LUNDY'S TRUE 'OLD LIGHT'.

The Old Light lighthouse on Lundy was literally built on the very site on Beacon Hill where once a 2nd - 4th Century Celtic Christian Community had been. Very little concrete history about the British church of this period is actually written down but it was definitely in existence and highly effective in spreading the authentic gospel throughout the Celtic fringes of the nation for the best part of 500 years prior to St Augustine's arrival in Canterbury. The Celtic church continued to exist in Britain beyond the Council of Whitby (664AD) but it gradually lost power as an increasingly Christianised society required a change of ministerial emphasis from an itinerant evangelistic model towards the pastoral one based on the parish system which the Roman model of church supplied and which we still know today.

God used the Celtic remains at the Old Light on Lundy, especially one early grave that is said to be that of St Patrick's grandfather Potitus, to direct us towards an exploration of the particular beliefs, practices and patterns of life in the British church of the 2nd - 4th centuries. This was a time when Britain was still pagan, governed by an oppressive Roman empire and the native British church persecuted.

These early British believers did not live in a large powerful medieval abbey with its wealth, strict order and ritual. Up to twelve individuals gathered together in loose association providing corporate reassurance, security and sometimes refuge for others. They lived off the land and slept in simple stone huts. A high value was placed on the kind of sincere friendship, open trust and strong fellowship-bond found amongst the biblical early church. The lifestyle was uncomplicated and informal. The spiritual teacher was appointed solely because of their inspiring wisdom, holiness and other gifts. Relationships were characterised by accountability, transparency and trust. These underground groups became hidden centres of worship, teaching, prayer and discipleship. The

Great Commission of Matthew 28: 18-20 and Mark 16:15-18 was taken very seriously which is why their humble itinerant lifestyle modelled that of Jesus and the apostles.

I hope you will agree with me that digging down into the roots of our native British church heritage reveals something of great value. These largely unknown but brave Celtic believers carried something in their spiritual D.N.A. which we need again today if the Light of Life is to be seen in the church as persecution grows. Like us they lived in uncertain times - the Roman Empire was retreating and the whole fabric of society was uncertain and under threat. Just as today the ordinary people at ground level were in need of rescue as society, as they knew it, began to crumble. Into this scenario the fearless Celts embodied a living Spirit-led organism, exhibited tremendous faith and saw God perform mighty miracles. They understood the spiritual realm as well as the natural and were serious, sober and obedient. These believers were not religious - that only came to the church after Whitby - but they simply walked in a daily intimate relationship of covenant fellowship with God and one another. Their hearts burned from the constant filling of the oil of the Spirit in their hearts as they carried the Light of Life, so bringing spiritual awakening to whole geographical areas of the South West of England and South Wales. Little by little God used this movement which had begun underground to change society.

Over the past six weeks together we have been journeying on this old or ancient way. It is not about us becoming Celts or romanticising their way but rather simply learning to walk, as they walked, as Jesus, Noah, Abraham, Moses and David walked, in covenant relationship with God. If we learn these lessons, we will with God's grace, be equipped to stand strong in God through the storms that lie ahead.

The following poem was written by Nicholas Szkiler at the end of our visit to Lundy in February 2019. It gives a fitting conclusion to our journey...

LUNDY'S ANCIENT LIGHT by Nicholas Szkiler.

Moonlight shadows on Lundy's rocky shore;

Unchanged from days of saints who walked before.

The fire not seen by most who tread these paths,

Pilgrims dug for embers from the past.

And now a beacon blazes once again;

Wind of Spirit fans the holy flame,

The hidden light we've been allowed to find.

The Saviour's Light to draw all humankind.

The deer, the lamb, the horse their quiet gaze,

Witness of the few who came to praise.

We know where this began, not where it ends;

The beacon light illuminates these isles again.